CONTEMPORARY LAWS AND ISSUES ON VIOLENCE AGAINST WOMEN AND GIRLS IN NIGERIA

Bibliografische Information der Deutschen Nationalbibliothek
Die Deutsche Nationalbibliothek verzeichnet diese Publikation in der Deutschen Nationalbibliografie; detaillierte bibliografische Daten sind im Internet über https://dnb.de abrufbar.

ISBN 978-3-96203-201-2 (Print)
ISBN 978-3-96203-202-9 (E-Book)

CONTEMPORARY LAWS AND ISSUES ON VIOLENCE AGAINST WOMEN AND GIRLS IN NIGERIA

Edited by:

Professor Joy Ngozi Ezeilo

Dr. Uchechukwu Nwoke

Dr. Ndubuisi Nwafor

GALDA VERLAG 2022

APPRECIATION

We thank Action Aid Nigeria (AAN), Women's Voice and Leadership (WVL) projects funded by Global Affairs Canada (GAC) for supporting the Police Conference and Training Workshop that led to the production of this book.

NOTES ON CONTRIBUTORS

1. **Joy Ngozi Ezeilo**, is a Law Professor and Dean Emeritus, Faculty of Law, University of Nigeria, Nsukka. She holds a Ph.D. (Nig.), LLM (London), LL.B. (Nig.), BL, Diploma, Peace & Conflict Resolution (Uppsala). She served as the United Nations Special Rapporteur on trafficking in persons, especially women and children from 2008 to 2014. She served as a Member, United Nations Secretary General's Civil Society Advisory Board on Sexual Abuse and Exploitation (2019-2021). From 2013 to 2016, she was a member of the Board of Trustees for the United Nations Trust Fund for Victims of Trafficking managed by UNODC, Vienna, Austria. Prof. Ezeilo is a Member, the Body of Benchers, Nigeria and also, Member of the Governing Council of the Nigerian Institute of Advanced Legal Studies (NIALS). Professor Joy Ezeilo was a former Commissioner for Gender and Social Development, Enugu State and served also as a member of the Governing Council, Nigerian Institute of International Affairs (NIIA) from 2012 to 2015. She is active in the civil society and feminist movement and founded Women Aid Collective (WACOL) and Tamar Sexual Assault Referral Centre (Tamar SARC). Joy Ezeilo is the 2019 winner of the National Human Rights Award. She has also received several national and international awards, including being conferred with a Nigerian Government national honour of Officer of the Order of Niger (OON) in 2006 and recognized in April, 2013 by Newsweek/Daily Beast International Magazine, USA as one of the 125 women of impact in the world for her work, especially in combating human trafficking--a modern day slavery. She is also a recipient of the prestigious British Chevening scholarship (1995) and a grantee of the John D. and Catherine T. MacArthur Foundation's Funds for Leadership Development (1998). She is also a recipient of Hon. Justice Taslim Elias Award (2019). Prof. Ezeilo pioneered the teaching of Women, Children and the Law at the University of Nigeria in 1997 as well contributed significantly to the curriculum for the teaching of health law and reproductive rights adopted by both National Universities Commission (NUC) and the Nigerian Association of Law

Teachers (NALT). She has been at the forefront of the passage of many laws in Nigeria, including the Violence Against Persons Act (2015) and the Enugu State equivalent in 2019. She is a legal and development consultant to many international organizations, including United Nation agencies. She is currently the Deputy Chairperson of the African Women's Leadership Network (AWLN) Nigerian chapter and also a Member of the Enugu State Judicial Panel of Inquiry on Police Brutality and Extra-Judicial Killings.

2. **Hon. Justice Comfort Chinyere Ani Ph.D., MCIArb** obtained her LL. B degree from the Nnamdi Azikiwe University in 1990. Justice Ani was called to the Nigeria Bar in 1991 and obtained a Master's Degree in Law, LL.M from the University of Nigeria, Nsukka in 1997. In 2009, she obtained a Ph.D. in Public law from the University of Lagos. Her Lordship was appointed Judge of the High Court of Enugu State in 2015. She has delivered over 300 landmark judgments and rulings on several recondite arrears of the law. Before joining the Bench, she was a Senior Research Fellow and Head of Department Akinola Aguda School of Postgraduate Studies, Nigerian Institute of Advanced Legal Studies (NIALS). She has co-edited two books and published more than 35 articles in reputable journals and books.

3. **Uchechukwu Nwoke** is a Senior Lecturer and the current Head, Department of Commercial and Corporate Law, Faculty of Law, University of Nigeria, Enugu Campus. He graduated with an LLB Degree from the Faculty of Law, University of Nigeria (Enugu Campus). Uchechukwu obtained an LL.M in International Trade Law from the University of Wales (United Kingdom) and a PhD in Law from the Kent Law School, University of Kent (United Kingdom). Uchechukwu joined the Faculty of Law, University of Nigeria as a lecturer in 2016 and teaches Jurisprudence, Criminal Law and Private International Law at the undergraduate level; Corporate Theory and Governance, as well as Commercial Law at the Postgraduate level. Uchechukwu has published scholarly articles in his chosen subject areas, and his research interests are in the areas of International Commercial Law, Corporate Theory and Governance, Criminal Law, Jurisprudence, Human Rights Law and Private International Law.

4. **Amucheazi Chibike Oraeto** is a lecturer at the Faculty of Law of University of Nigeria with special interest in commercial law, Jurisprudence and global laws on human rights. He has published widely in these areas of law and has keen interest in the development of the African legislative frameworks and governance. Amucheazi focuses on global peace through development of viable laws and is currently on a PhD study with research focus on a workable legal form for self-determination in Nigeria. Amucheazi attended the University of South Wales, United Kingdom where he obtained his LLM in International Commercial Law with a distinction.

5. **Ndubuisi Augustine Nwafor**, LL.B (Uyo), LL.M (Glasgow Caledonian University), PhD (Stirling, Scotland) is a Senior Lecturer and the Head of Department of Jurisprudence and Legal Theory. He is also the Associate Dean of the Faculty of Law, University of Nigeria Enugu Campus. His research and teaching interests include international commercial law, trade law, economic law, human rights and ocean/marine law;

6. **Solo Akpanufot** is a development consultant and a doctoral research student with the institute for development studies, University of Nigeria. He has over 12 years cognate experience in working with international development agencies, state and non-state actors in the area of community policing, justice and security sector reform, educational management, institutional development, water, sanitation and hygiene (WASH) and development research. He has received many awards for his contribution to effective policing in Nigeria. Until 31st March 2020, he was the Enugu State Intervention Lead (SIL) of the Nigeria Policing Programme (NPP). He could be reached via email on *soladestiny@yahoo.com*.

7. **Obinna James Edeh** is a lecturer in the Department of Public Law, Faculty of Law, and University of Nigeria. Prior to the present engagement, he served as a staff researcher and consultant at the Development Strategy Centre and Council on African Security and Development respectively. He has also served as an intern/staff lawyer at the Office of the Legal Adviser, Organization for the Prohibition of Chemical Weapons (OPCW), The Hague, Netherlands. Obinna attended the University of

Northampton in England where he obtained a Masters of Laws degree in International Criminal Law and Security. He is also an alumnus of The Hague Academy of International Law (Netherlands) and the University of Nigeria respectively. He has consulted for the Deutsche Gesellschaft für Internationale Zusammenarbeit (GIZ), The African Association of International Law, and the Afri-heritage Institute, and for the United Nations Development Programme. Obinna is a grant recipient from the Raoul Wallenberg Institute of Human Rights and Humanitarian Law, Lund University, Sweden. He has published and presented research papers within and outside Nigeria. He is currently teaching Constitutional Law, Children and Women's Law (CHIWIL), International Human Rights Law and Health Law. Obinna has research interests in International Human Rights and Humanitarian Law, National Security and Rule of Law with a growing interest in Health Law.

8. **Uju Peace Okeke** is a lawyer, Human Rights activist, gender researcher, reproductive and sexual health expert, Notary Public and professional negotiator and mediator. She lectures at the Faculty of Law, University of Nigeria, Enugu Campus (UNEC). She obtained Bachelor of Laws Degree from Obafemi Awolowo University Ile-Ife, Osun State, Nigeria and and Masters Degree in Law, Human Rights (specialising in Reproductive and Sexual Health Rights) from the University of the Free State, Bloemfontein South Africa. With infectious passion, she lends her voice to constitutional, political, business, leadership, cultural issues, and human rights of women, children, elderly, migrants and PWDs through research, writing, litigation and advocacy.

9. **Daniel Ikechukwu Onyeonagu** was called to the Nigerian Bar in 2009 after obtaining his Bachelor of Laws Degree from University of Nigeria. He later obtained a Master of Laws Degree from International University Bamenda, Cameroon. He served in Paul C. Ananaba (SAN) & Co. as a legal Practitioner where he distinguished himself in legal practice. He was a Governorship Candidate in his State in the 2015 general election and was elected the National Legal Adviser of one of the political parties in Nigeria in 2016, a position he held till 2017 before joining Faculty of Law, University of Nigeria as a lecturer. He is the Principal partner of Dan Onyeonagu & Co., a fast growing law firm. Dan is an unrepentant

human rights activist. He teaches Criminal Law, Human Rights Law and Intellectual Property Law.

10. **Ijeoma Chinaka Ezeude** is a lawyer with fourteen years (14) post call to Bar experience. She graduated from the University of Nigeria, with a Second Class Upper Division in 2006. She is the Head of Legal Unit of Women's Aid Collective (WACOL) and Tamar Sexual Assault Referral Centre that offers free legal aid and other integrated services to women and children. She leads a team of pro bono lawyers actively involved in providing legal assistance and support to victims/survivors of gender based violence. She has handled and supervised over 1000 cases since joining WACOL. Ijeoma has a Master of Laws (LL.M) degree acquired in 2015 and is currently a Ph.D. student of the University of Nigeria. In addition to her work at the Legal Clinic, she also handles some programmes on women's human rights and empowerment of girls. She oversees the Women Voices and Leadership Project (WVL) in partnership with Global Affairs Canada and Action Aid Nigeria.

11. **Dr. Obiajulu Nnamuchi** is former head, Department of Public Law, Faculty of Law, University of Nigeria (Enugu Campus), with teaching duties also at the College of Medicine and Faculty of Health Sciences. He specializes in human rights, bioethics, public health and medical law. He obtained a basic law degree/LL.B from UNIZIK (Awka), LL.M. International Human Rights Law (Notre Dame), LL.M. Health Law and Policy (Toronto), LL.M. International Law (Lund), M.A. Bioethics and Medical Humanities (Louisville), and S.J.D/PhD, Health Law and Policy (Loyola, Chicago). A research fellow at the Institute for Bioethics, Health Policy and Law at the University of Louisville School of Medicine (2007 – 2009) and Beazley Institute for Health Law and Policy, Loyola University Chicago Law School (2006 – 2011), Dr. Nnamuchi's scholarly interests are mainly focused on the intersection of law, bioethics and medicine; human rights; global health; and health governance and financing – areas on which he has written extensively. Currently working on the interface between law and communicable diseases, particularly in the realm of tobacco control and regulation, his publication has appeared in top journals such as Journal of Law, Medicine and Ethics; Human Rights Quarterly; Journal of Medicine

and Law; Journal of Health and Biomedical Law; Developing World Bioethics; Annals of Health Law and Life Sciences and so forth. Together with Prof. Brigit Toebes (foremost global authority on the right to health) and colleagues, Dr. Nnamuchi is the editor of "The Right to Health: A Multi-Country Study of Law, Police and Practice," a leading treatise on the subject. Perhaps, more importantly, he is amongst the authors of "Comparative Health Law and Policy: Critical Perspectives on Nigerian and Global Health Law" – the first comprehensive and most authoritative textbook on key issues relating to health law and policy in Nigeria.

TABLE OF CONTENTS

CONTEMPORARY LAWS AND ISSUES ON VIOLENCE AGAINST WOMEN AND GIRLS IN NIGERIA

Introduction

Violence is present in the very structure of the universe. Perhaps, there has been no age or civilisation without violence. Worldwide, women are disproportionately affected by gender-based violence, thus, necessitating the focus on "violence against women and girls". Women and girls in Nigeria face different levels of sexual and gender-based violence in both private and public life, often without protection from the law. Compounding the problem of women and their rights is Nigeria's pluralist legal system, which includes Customary and Sharia Laws that often reinforce sex stereotypes, including giving a man the right to batter the wife or make decisions on her behalf. Violence against women and girls (VAWG), also known as gender-based violence and sexual and gender-based violence (SGBV) are violent acts the victims of which are primarily or exclusively women or girls. Violence against women infringes on and impairs the enjoyment by women of their human rights and fundamental freedoms.

In view of the growing prevalence of violence against women and girls in Nigeria, Women Aid Collective (WACOL) continues to deem it imperative to work towards the elimination of all forms of violence against women and girls. The civil society organisation (CSO) has organised seminars and conferences to train stakeholders in the area of preventing violence against women and girls. This edited book collection is a product of one of these training sessions, organised for Police officers on September 17, 2020 at Dannic Hotels, Enugu. This edited collection is a compilation of some of the papers presented at the seminar.

In the first paper in the collection, Justice Comfort Chinyere Ani of the Enugu State High Court, discussed the Enugu State Violence against Persons Prohibition Law, 2019. The paper, while highlighting the various provision of the Law, argued that it buttresses some existing criminal provisions, while also addressing the gaps in existing laws. Justice Ani also contends that the provisions of the Enugu State law were crafted bearing in mind the States' peculiar traditional repugnant, and sometimes harmful, cultural practices.

In her own contribution, Professor Joy Ngozi Ezeilo traced the historical facts surrounding the passing into law of the Violence against Persons (Prohibition) Act by the National Assembly in 2015. She contends that the Act commendably covers most of the prevalent forms of violence that could be categorised into: physical violence; psychological violence; sexual violence; harmful traditional practices; and socio-economic violence. Specifically, she writes that the VAPP Act comprehensively dealt with one of the most vexed forms of sexual violence – rape – which under existing penal laws protects only females and is limited to vaginal penetration. The Act has expanded the scope of rape to protect males and to include anal and oral sex as well as protect the identity of rape victims.

Dr Uchechukwu Nwoke undertook a comparative analysis of the Federal Violence against Persons (Prohibition) Act (2015) and the Enugu State Violence against Persons Prohibition Law, 2019. The paper, while undertaking this comparative analysis, attempts to sensitise the police and other law enforcement agents on the two laws on violence against persons (especially women and girls) in order to help strengthen the capacity of these law enforcement agents to provide effective responses to victims of violence.

Chibuike Amucheazi (Esq.) looked at the theme of violence from the perspective of sexual assault, which, according to him, has become a reoccurring horror show for women in Nigeria. While applauding the domestication of the VAPP law in Enugu State, his contribution points out some apparent shortcomings of the Law, centred essentially on the protection of women in sexual assaults. He argues that the subsistence of certain legal materials such as police methods of investigation and general attitude still impacts negatively on prosecution of sexual assault cases.

In the fifth paper of the collection, Dr Ndubuisi Nwafor examined the powers of the Police under the Enugu State VAPP Law (2019). He approached this through the prism of evidence preservation, fact finding and interrogation in cases of violence against women and girls. In his conclusion, he argues that the police, in order to effectively administer the Enugu State VAPP Law, should desist from excessive and unreasonable use of force in their law enforcement duties.

Mr. Solomon Akpanufot looked at the critical role that police officers play as first responders in violence offences. According to him, police officers are the first actors who a victim of sexual and gender-based violence (SGBV) is most likely to approach for succor. In this context, he discusses some conventional roles the police can play in issues of SGBV and suggests practical steps which could be taken to build confidence and prevent the re-victimisation of victims.

While making his own contribution, Mr Obinna Ede (Esq.) placed the Enugu State VAPP Law 2019 side by side with international and national human rights instruments relative to women and girls, to see how to bring the former at par with global norms and strengthen the effectiveness of its implementation.

Relying on the Violence against Persons Prohibition Act (2015) and Violence against Persons Prohibition Law of Enugu State (2019), Uju Peace Okeke (Esq.) discussed the meaning, forms, and elements of physical and sexual violence with their human rights dimension. Applauding the holistic protection guaranteed in these laws, she concludes that in the absence of implementation fueled by purposeful awareness, the desire for a violence-free Nigeria will remain illusory.

In Chapter 10, Daniel Onyeonagu (Esq.) contended that despite decades of feminist activism, and avalanche of laws to tame the scourge of rape, the menace continues to escalate at appalling rates. He explored the challenges of prosecuting rape cases in Nigeria and concluded with recommendations on ways and means of tackling this social menace in Nigeria.

The last contribution (chapter 11) grapples with one of the more recent controversial topics in human rights literature. The chapter examines whether it is an overreach for the VAPP law of Enugu State to not only classify all forms of female genital ritual (FGR) as encapsulated within the term "harmful traditional practices" but also impose a blanket ban on the procedure, regardless of consent of the part of mature, rational and competent women. Delving deep into extant literature to examine the health consequences (or lack thereof) of the procedure as well as the opinion of women in practising communities, Nnamuchi urges that the FGR prohibitory tentacles of Enugu State VAPP law should be revisited.

AN OVERVIEW OF THE ENUGU STATE VIOLENCE AGAINST PERSONS (PROHIBITION) LAW, 2019

PROTOCOL

I must first start by expressing my heartfelt appreciation to the Executive Director of Women Aid Collective (WACOL), Professor Joy N. Ezeilo (OON), who found me worthy enough to deliver this keynote paper at this gathering of distinguished Police officers. I will not fail to commend WACOL for championing the advancement and protection of human rights, especially that of the vulnerable ones in our society, such as women and children. As usual WACOL is blazing the trail in the sensitisation and education of stakeholders on this novel Law, the Enugu State Violence Against Persons (Prohibition) Law, 2019.

This training comes at a very critical point in our society where offences involving violence against persons is on the increase, especially offences involving sexual violence such as rape and defilement. It is my belief that at the end of this training, the participants will be enriched and well equipped intellectually to enforce this new law.

INTRODUCTION

Nigeria as a country and Enugu as a state has at the federal and state levels respectively, enacted legislations on human rights, rights of the child, child protection, marriage and widowhood. Our extant criminal laws hitherto outlaw violence, assault, rape, defilement, human trafficking, kidnapping, etc. Nigeria, being a member of United Nations, is signatory to major treaties on the rights of the child and on discrimination and violence against women. Nevertheless, we have our peculiar cultural and traditional nuances that have not been adequately addressed by the existing legislations and international and regional instruments. The

Enugu State Violence Against Person Prohibition Law, 2019, whereas it buttresses some existing criminal provisions, in addition, addresses the gaps in the existing laws, while its provisions are crafted in line with our peculiar traditional repugnant, and sometimes harmful, cultural practices.

This Law makes copious and essential provisions that aim at addressing the emerging dimensions of some contemporary societal ills that were not hitherto covered by the extant legislations. Where some of them are hitherto provided, the definition may not be adequately encompassing or the penalties are not stringent enough to have the required deterrent effect, given the prevalence of the wrong in our society. Besides stringent penalties, this new Law provides enhanced remedies for victims of these practices who have been more or less neglected before now. Some of the commendable and unique provisions of this law include:

- Inclusion of males as capable of being victims of sexual offences
- Outlawing female circumcision with adequate penalty upon infraction
- Provisions against Spousal/partner battery
- Provisions against forceful ejection of spouse from home
- Provisions against emotional, verbal and psychological abuse
- Provisions against abandonment of spouse, children and dependants, etc.
- Establishment of Agency on Violence Against Persons

Arrangement of Parts, Sections and Forms

This Law is arranged into five parts broken into 45 Sections. There are also six Forms annexed in the Schedule of the Law. A summary of the arrangement is as follows:

Part 1 – Citation and Interpretation (Sections 1 and 2).

Part 2 – Offences (Sections 3 to 22).

Part 3- Jurisdiction of the Court (Sections 23 to 35).

Part 4- Service providers (Sections 36 to 39).

Part 5- Regulatory Body (Sections 40 to 45).

Form 1- Application for Protection Order.

Form 2- Application for protection order by a person other than the victim.

Form 3- Affidavit in support of Application for protection order.

Form 4- Consent to Application for protection order.

Form 5 General form on interim protection order.

Form 6- General form of protection order.

PART 1 - CITATION AND INTERPRETATION

The Law is to be cited as the Enugu State Violence Against Persons (Prohibition) Law, 2019. It is deemed to have come into effect on the 4th day of April, 2019.

By the short title of this law, which is the Enugu State Violence Against Persons (Prohibition) Law, 2019, it is clear that the law outrightly prohibits or forbids violence against any person, both male and female, rich or poor and young or old in Enugu State. The long title of this law states:

> *"A Law to Eliminate Violence in Private and Public Life, Prohibit all forms of violence including Physical, Sexual, Psychological, Domestic, Harmful Traditional Practices; Discrimination against Persons and to Provide Maximum Protection and Effective Remedies for Victims and Punishment of Offenders and other Matters Related Thereto".*

The long title brings out more detailed import of this Law. From the long title, it is apparent that this Law is geared towards eliminating all forms of violence both in private and public life. It confronts all forms of violence such as physical, sexual, psychological, domestic, harmful traditional practices as well as discrimination against persons. The Law also sets out to provide maximum protection and effective remedies for victims of violence and also sets out punishments for offenders.

Section 2 defines or gives the meaning of the following words and phrases that feature in the law such as: Abandonment of women, children and other persons; accredited service provider; Arm; Circumcision of a girl or woman; Civil proceeding; Dangerous weapon; Domestic Relationship; Domestic violence; Economic abuse; Emergency monetary relief; Emotional, Verbal and psychological abuse; Forced isolation from family and friends; Harassment; Harmful Traditional Practices; Perpetrators; Indecent exposure; Intimidation; Physical Abuse; Protection officer, Sexual abuse; Sexual assault; Sexual exploitation; Sexual harassment; Sexual intimidation; Spousal/partner battery, Stalking; Substance attack; Trafficking; Victim; Violence; Violence perpetrated by non-state actors and Vulnerable groups.

PART 2 - OFFENCES

1. Rape

The offence of rape is defined in Section 3 as follows:

1) A person commits the offence of rape if

a. He intentionally penetrates the vagina, anus or mouth of another person no matter how slight with his sex organ or any part of his body or anything else

b. The other person does not consent to the penetration; or

c. The consent is obtained by force or means of threat or intimidation of any kind or by fear of harm or by means of false and fraudulent representation as to the nature of the act or the use of any substance or addictive capable of taking away the will of such person or in the case of a married person by impersonating his spouse or partner.

The definition of the offence of rape in this Law is commendable and an improvement on the definition of rape under Section 308 of the Criminal Code Law of Enugu State. The definition in Section 3 of this Law is wider, more elaborate and more inclusive. The definition in Section 308 of the Criminal Code excludes some sexual offences involving oral or anal penetration with objects. The definition of the offence of rape under this new Law is without discrimination as to gender of the victim. In other words, both male and female may be victim of rape by the definition given under Section 3 of this Law. The offence can be committed by not only penetrating the vagina with a sex organ, but also involves penetration of the anus or mouth no matter how slight with a sex organ or any part of the body or anything else.

Punishment for the offence of rape is prescribed under Section 4 as imprisonment for life. Where the offender is below 18 years old, he shall be remanded in a remand home or appropriate place for a number of years as the judge deems fit.

It is observed that there is no provision in this law for attempted rape. The Criminal Code provides for attempted rape and makes it punishable by 14 years imprisonment. Perhaps, prosecutors may have to charge suspects of attempted rape under the Criminal Code since there is no such provision in this new Law.

It is to be noted that upon conviction for rape, the Judge does not have any discretion to exercise as regards the terms of imprisonment as the law prescribes a mandatory life imprisonment, except where the defendant is less than 18 years. The seriousness of the penalty attached to the offence of rape will invariably make the judges circumspect in analysing evidence and ensuring that the threshold of proof beyond reasonable doubt is achieved before conviction. This should place a serious burden on investigators and prosecutors to be very diligent in their duties so as to satisfy the requirement of proof beyond reasonable doubt required for conviction, otherwise, where there is any doubt as to the evidence of the prosecution, the doubt will be resolved in favour of the defendant.

2. Inflicting Physical Injury on a Person

Section 5 creates the offence of wilfully causing or inflicting physical injury on another person by means of any weapon, substance or object. The offence is punishable upon conviction by a term of imprisonment not exceeding five years or a fine not exceeding N100,000.00 or to both fine and imprisonment.

3. Coercion

Section 6 creates the offence of Coercion. Any person who coerces another to engage in any act to the detriment of that other person's physical or psychological well-being commits an offence and upon conviction is liable to three years imprisonment.

4. Wilfully Placing a Person in Fear of Physical Injury.

By Section 7, a person who wilfully or knowingly places a person in fear of physical injury commits an offence and is liable on conviction to imprisonment for a term not exceeding two years or to a fine not exceeding N100,000 or to both fine and imprisonment.

5. Offensive Conduct

Section 8 provides that any person who compels another person by force or threat to engage in any conduct or act, sexual or otherwise, to the detriment of the victim's physical or psychological well-being commit an offence and is liable on conviction to imprisonment for a term not exceeding three years or to a fine not exceeding N100,000 or to both fine and imprisonment.

6. Performing Female Circumcision or Genital Mutilation

Just like the Child Rights Act and Law, this Law again outrightly prohibits and criminalises female circumcision or genital mutilation, which is a practice that is fraught with many negative health consequences for the victims. Section 9 (2) of this Law states that: Any person who performs female genital circumcision or genital mutilation, or engages another to carry out such circumcision or mutilation, commits an offence and is liable on conviction to imprisonment for a term not exceeding four years or a fine not exceeding N200,000 or to both fine and imprisonment. Both the person that performs the circumcision and the person that engages another to perform it, most likely a parent, are all liable and punishment is same for both.

Under Section 2 of this law, circumcision of a girl or woman means cutting off all or part of the external sex organ of a girl or woman other than on medical ground.

7. Forceful Ejection of Partner

This unique and novel provision is a very welcome development in our law. Section 10 criminalises the act of forcefully ejecting a partner or denying access to a partner. It provides that any marriage partner who forcefully evicts his or her partner from her home or refuses him or her access therein commits an offence and is liable on conviction to imprisonment for a term not exceeding two years or a fine not exceeding N50,000 or to both fine and imprisonment liable. This provision will help to curb the abusive situation where by a spouse is denied access into his or her matrimonial home by his or her spouse because of a matrimonial quarrel.

8. Economic Abuse

This is another unique and novel provision, which further reinforces the constitutional provision on right to freedom from discrimination and right to own immovable property enshrined in Sections 41 and 42 respectively, of the Constitution of the Federal Republic of Nigeria, 1999, as amended.

Section 11 of the Law provides that any person who commits economic abuse of another commits an offence and is liable on conviction to imprisonment for a term not exceeding two years or a fine not exceeding N200,000 or to both fine and imprisonment liable.

Economic abuse is defined in Section 2 to mean denial of inheritance or succession rights, the unrestricted deprivation of economic and financial resources to which any person is entitled or which any person requires out of necessity, including household necessities, mortgage bond repayment or payment of rent in respect of a shared residence; the unreasonable disposal or destruction of household effects or other property in which any person has interest.

In the case of **Ukeje v. Ukeje, (2014) 11 NWLR (Pt. 1418) 384**, Rhodes Vivour JSC held that no matter the circumstances of the birth of a female child, such a child is entitled to an inheritance from her late father's estate. "Consequently, the Igbo customary law which disentitles a female child from partaking in the sharing of her deceased father's estate is in breach of Section 42(1) and (2) of the Constitution, a fundamental rights provision guaranteed to every Nigerian. His Lordship went ahead to declare the said discriminatory customary law void as it conflicts with Section 42(1) and (2) of the Constitution. Also in the case of **Anekwe v. Nweke, SC 129/2013, (2014) LPELR- 22697 (SC)**, Clara Bata Ogunbiyi JSC, reading the lead judgement held inter alia:

> *I hasten to add at this point that the custom and practices of Awka people upon which the appellants have relied for their counter-claim is hereby outrightly*

> *condemned in very strong terms. In other words, a custom of this nature in the 21st century societal setting will only tend to depict the absence of the realities of human civilisation. It is punitive, uncivilised and only intended to protect the selfish perpetration of male dominance which is aimed at suppressing the right of the womenfolk in the given society. One would expect that the days of such obvious differential discrimination are over. Any culture that disinherits a daughter from her father's estate or wife from her husband's property by reason of God instituted gender differential should be punitively and decisively dealt with.*

See also the case of **Nzekwu v. Nzekwu (1989) 3 SCNJ 167**.

9. Forced Isolation or Separation from Family and Friends

Section 12 provides that any person who forcefully isolates another from family and friends commits an offence and is liable on conviction to imprisonment for a term not exceeding six months or a fine not exceeding N100,000 or to both fine and imprisonment liable.

This section is somehow similar to Section 316 of the Criminal Code. Section 316 makes it an offence punishable with two years imprisonment for any person to unlawfully confine or detain another in any place against his will or to unlawfully deprive another of his personal liberty.

10. Causing Emotional, Verbal and Psychological Abuse

Section 13 criminalises causing emotional, verbal and psychological abuse on another commits an offence and is liable on conviction to imprisonment for a term not exceeding 1 year or a fine not exceeding N100,000 or to both fine and imprisonment liable.

11. Subjecting a Widow to Harmful Widowhood Practices

Section 14 states that any person who subjects a widow to harmful traditional practices commits an offence and is liable on conviction to imprisonment for a term not exceeding two years or a fine not exceeding N200,000 or to both fine and imprisonment liable.

Section 2 defines "harmful traditional practices" as all traditional behaviour, attitudes, and /or practices, which negatively affect the fundamental rights of any person and includes harmful widowhood practices as provided in Section 3 (1) (a-j) of the Prohibition of the Infringement of Widows and Widowers Fundamental Rights Law, 2001, denial of inheritance or succession rights, female genital mutilation or female circumcision, forced marriage and forced isolation from family and friends.

The harmful widowhood practices enumerated in Section 3 (1) (a-j) of the Prohibition of the Infringement of Widows and Widowers Fundamental Rights Law, 2001, Cap. 124 Laws of Enugu State include:

a. To permit the hairs on the head or any other part of the body to be shaved;
b. To sleep either alone or on the same bed or be locked in a room with corpse of the husband/wife;
c. Not to receive condolence visits from sympathisers during the period of mourning;
d. To be re-married by a relative of the late husband/wife;
e. To sit on the floor or be naked during any period of the husband's/ wife's burial rites;
f. To drink the water used in washing the corpse of the husband/wife;
g. To weep and wail loudly at intervals at any time after the death of the husband/wife except at one's own volition or involuntary action;
h. To remain in confinement after the death of the husband/wife for any given period;
i. To vacate the matrimonial home;
j. To do any other thing which contravenes the fundamental rights entrenched in the Constitution or is degrading the person.

Punishment for contravening the provisions of the Cap. 124 Laws of Enugu State is a fine of five thousand Naira or imprisonment for two years; this new Law, the Enugu State Violence Against Persons (Prohibition) Law, retained the two years punishment for subjecting a widow to harmful widowhood practice, but increased the fine from a paltry N5,000 to N200,000 or both fine and imprisonment.

11. Abandonment of Spouse Children and other Dependants without Sustenance.

Section 15 makes it an offence for a person to abandon a wife/husband, children or other dependant without any means of sustenance and is punishable on conviction to imprisonment for a term not exceeding 3 years or a fine not exceeding N250,000 or to both fine and imprisonment.

12. Stalking

By Section 16, any person who stalks another person commits an offence and is liable on conviction to imprisonment for a term not exceeding one year or a fine not exceeding N100,000 or to both fine and imprisonment liable.

Stalking is defined in Section 2 as repeatedly watching or loitering outside of or near the building or place where such person resides, works, carries on business, studies or happens to be; or repeatedly following, pursuing or accosting any person in a manner, which induces fear or anxiety.

13. Intimidation of Person

It is an offence under Section 17 for a person to intimidate another person. It is punishable on conviction to one year imprisonment or fine of N200,000 or both fine and imprisonment.

14. Spousal/Partner Battery

Any person who batters his spouse commits an offence under Section 18 and is punishable on conviction to one year imprisonment or fine of N200,000 or both fine and imprisonment. This offence can be committed by either a wife or a husband.

15. Carrying out Harmful Traditional Practice on Another

Under Section 19 any person who carries out harmful traditional practices on another commits an offence punishable with four years imprisonment or a fine of N100,000 or both imprisonment and fine.

16. Substance Attack

Section 20 provides that any person who uses chemical, biological or any other harmful liquid on another commits an offence, which is punishable on conviction with life imprisonment without option of fine.

This provision is to curb situations where a person sometimes permanently injures and deforms another person by pouring harmful liquid such as acid, hot water, etc. Such cases were dealt with hitherto by charging the offender for causing grievous harm under Section 288 (g) of the Criminal Code of Enugu State. The Criminal Code provides punishment for unlawfully casting or throwing corrosive liquid or any such substance upon any person to be life imprisonment.

17. Administering Substance

Under Section 21, it is an offence to intentionally administer a substance or to cause a substance to be administered to or be taken by another with the intention of stupefying or overpowering that person to enable the person engage in a sexual activity with that person. The offence is punishable with a term of imprisonment not exceeding 10 years or fine of N50,000.00 or both imprisonment and fine.

The fine prescribed for this offence is low, considering the term of imprisonment prescribed, when compared with the other offences. For instance, spousal battery, under section 18, is punishable by imprisonment for one year and fine not exceeding N200,000. Abandonment of Spouse, Children and other Dependants without Sustenance, under Section 15, attracts punishment of three years or fine of N250, 000.

18. Indecent Exposure

This occurs when any person intentionally exposes his or her genital organ or a substantial part thereof with the intention of causing distress to the other party or that another person seeing it may be tempted or induced to commit an offence under this Law. This offence is punishable with a term of imprisonment not exceeding one year or fine of N50,000.

All the offences in this Law, except rape, also have punishments for attempting to commit the offence, inciting, aiding, abetting, counselling and assisting in the commission of the offence. The punishment for these class of offenders is invariably, half of the prison term of the completed offence and half of the fine. Another striking thing is that, except for rape, great discretion is given to the Judge or Magistrate in sentencing. The terms of imprisonment is such that the Judge or Magistrate is not to exceed the stated term of imprisonment or the stated fine, meaning that the Judge or Magistrate may go lower, using his discretion. The Judge or Magistrate is also allowed discretion in deciding whether to impose imprisonment or fine, or both.

PART 3- JURISDICTION OF COURT

By section 23, only the High Court or Magistrate Court in the State has jurisdiction to hear and grant applications brought under this Law. Under Section 24, application for a Protection Order may be brought to the Court following a complaint of violence. The application can be made by the complainant or on his or her behalf by any other person such as a police officer, protection officer, accredited service provider, counsellor, health service provider, social worker or teacher, who has interest in the well-being of the complainant. The application has to be with the written consent of the complainant except if the complainant is a minor, mentally retarded, unconscious or a person who is unable to provide the required consent.

The Court is empowered under Section 27 to make Protection Orders prohibiting the Respondent from the following:

Committing any act of domestic violence; enlisting the help of another to commit any such act; entering a shared household; entering complainant's residence or place of employment, alienating or disposing shared household or encumbering same; committing any other act as specified in the protection order. The Court can also make order as regards: seizure of any arm or dangerous weapon; for police officer to accompany the complainant to a specified place to assist in collecting personal property; order temporary relocation to a safer place approve mediation, etc.

The Protection Order can be varied, set aside or discharged upon application to the Court as provided under Sections 31 and 32. The Commissioner, the Applicant or the Respondent can apply to the Court to discharge the order.

Punishment for contravening an interim protection order is stated in Section 33 as a term of imprisonment not exceeding six months or a fine of N200,000 or both

Section 28 is on Police duties and powers. A police officer at the scene of violence has the duty to do the following:

a. Assist victim of violence to file a complaint

b. Provide or arrange safe transport for victim to an alternative residence, safe place or shelter where it is required

c. Provide or arrange transportation of victim to nearest hospital or medical facility where that is needed

d. Explain to the victim his rights to protection against violence and remedies under this Law

e. Explain to the victim that he has the right to lodge a criminal complaint in addition to any remedy under this Law

f. Accompany the victim to his or her residence to collect belongings

The Police is further empowered in section 28 (2) in addition to the powers under the Police Act, to arrest without a warrant any person he suspects on reasonable grounds to have committed an offence under Part 2 of this Law or any person against whom a complaint has been lodged.

Victims' Rights

Victim is defined in Section 2 as any person or persons who, individually or collectively, have suffered harm, including physical or mental injury, emotional suffering, economic loss or substantial impairment of their fundamental rights through acts or omissions that are in violation of this Law and/or the criminal laws of the Country. The term, 'Victim' also refers to the immediate family or dependants of the direct victim and any other person who has suffered harm in intervening to assist victims in distress.

Rights of victims are provided for in section 35. Rights of victims enumerated include:

a. The right to receive the necessary materials, medical, psychological, social and legal assistance through governmental agencies and non-governmental agencies providing such assistance

b. Right to rehabilitation and re-integration programme of the State to enable victims acquire skills in any vocation of the victim's choice and necessary formal education or access to credit facilities

Court Proceedings to be in Camera

Section 35 of the law limits the persons that can be in attendance in any proceedings in terms of this law. Only the following persons are allowed to be present during proceedings:

1. Officers of the court
2. Parties to the proceedings
3. Any person bringing application on behalf of the complainant
4. Legal practitioners representing any party in the proceeding
5. Accredited service provider
6. Witnesses
7. Not more than three persons to provide support for the complainant and the respondent, respectively
8. Any other person permitted by the court

PART 4- SERVICE PROVIDERS

It is provided under Section 36 that a voluntary association registered under the Companies and Allied Matters Act 1990 by the Corporate Affairs Commission (CAC) with the objectives of protecting the rights and interest of victims of violence shall register itself with the State Government as a service provider for the purpose of this law.

Duties of the Appropriate Government Agency

Section 36 (2) enjoins the Appropriate Government Agency to keep a register of all accredited service providers and circulate same to all police stations, Protection Officers and the court. The agency is also required to draw up guidelines for the operation of the accredited service providers.

Under Section 37, the appropriate Government Agency is to appoint Protection Officers in each Local Government Council as it may consider necessary to co-ordinate the activities of the police and the Accredited Service Providers in the Local Government Council.

The Protection Officers so appointed are to do the following:

Ensure that victims and supervisors have access to accredited service providers; access to transportation to alternative residence or a safe shelter, nearest hospital or medical facility; that victims are able to collect their belongings or properties from shared household or their residence; are able to get every possible assistance as ordered by the court in the protection Order on the respondent.

Duties of the Service Providers

Service providers have some duties under Section 36 (3) such as:

a. To record the incidence of violence reported if the aggrieved person so desired and forward a copy to the Magistrate and Protection Officer in the jurisdiction where the violence took place

b. Get aggrieved person medically examined and forward a copy of the medical report to the protection officer and the police station within the locality where the violence took place

c. Ensure that aggrieved person is provided shelter in a shelter home, if she so requires and forward report on that to the police in the locality

Section 36(4) excludes liability to legal prosecution and legal proceedings for service providers acting under this Law for anything done in good faith while discharging their functions under this Law.

Section 38 provides that the body vested with the regulation of this Law shall appoint a person as the Co-ordinator of the prevention of domestic violence. He shall submit annual reports to the State Government on the implementation of this Law and deposit a copy with the National Bureau for Statistics.

Section 39 provides that a court may declare a person a dangerous sexual offender if:

a) he has been convicted for a sexual offence more than once

b) Convicted of a sexual offence, which was accompanied with grievous harm or threat to life of the victim

c) he has been convicted of a sexual offence against a child

PART 5- REGULATORY BODY

Section 40 establishes a body to be known as the Agency on Violence Against Persons. The Agency shall be a legal personality capable of suing and being sued in its corporate name.

Section 41 mentions the functions of the Agency as follows:

a. Monitor and supervise the implementation of the provisions of this Law
b. Administer the operations of the Trust Fund
c. Provide and manage crises centres
d. Register accredited Service Providers, draw up guidelines of their operations and supervise their activities
e. Perform such other functions as may be specified by any law or enactment, and create directories of services
f. Recruit staff for the agency
g. Undertake such other activities as are necessary or expedient for giving full effect to the provisions of this Law
h. Co-ordinate the activities of the police and the accredited service providers, etc.

The composition of the Agency as provided by Section 42 of the Law includes:

a. A Chairman appointed by the Governor
b. Representative of the Commissioner of Police, not below the rank of a Superintendent of Police
c. The Ministry of Justice
d. The Ministry of Health
e. The Nigeria Prison Service
f. Two representatives of the Ministry of Women Affairs
g. An officer of the National Human Rights Commission
h. An officer of the Legal Aid Council
i. Four persons from the Legislative Advocacy Coalition on Violence Against Women
j. Two representatives from religious organisations
k. The Director General who shall be a woman and the Administrative Head of the Agency.

Section 43 specifies the quorum of the Agency at meetings to be one-third of the members. The Agency is empowered to disburse funds, appoint external auditors, oversee its own administration and engage in fund raising for the purpose of carrying out of its functions.

Finally, Section 45 establishes a Trust Fund for victims of violence against persons for the purpose of providing aid for the victims of violence.

CONCLUSION

The need for mass enlightenment on the provisions of this law cannot be over emphasised as ignorance of the law is not an excuse. It is recommended that this law be translated and printed out in simple Igbo language, which should be made accessible to schools, town unions, churches, etc. This law should be inculcated into the curriculum for police training at the Police College as well as made part of curriculum for continuous training of police men.

Various roles have been assigned to the government (through the Commissioner), the Courts, the non-governmental organisations and the Police. For instance, the victim has a right under this law to receive necessary material, medical, psychological, social and legal assistance, as well as take part in rehabilitation and reintegration programmes, etc. These roles require funding. Government should live up to the expectation of funding this initiative. International development partners can also leverage of this new law to fund non-governmental organisations that are poised to serve as service providers in actualising the intendment of this Law.

There is need for government to establish functional remand homes, where underaged offenders can upon conviction be remanded for their rehabilitation, education and training as provided under this Law as well as under the Child Rights Law. It is also of great importance for the Government to establish safe shelter homes for victims of violence as provided under Sections 28 and 36 (3) of this Law.

The Government is urged to urgently constitute the Regulatory Body as provided by Section 40 of this Law, that is, the Agency on Violence Against Persons, that will in turn appoint Protection Officers in each of the Local Government Councils as provided under Section 37 of this Law.

OVERVIEW OF THE VIOLENCE AGAINST PERSONS (PROHIBITION) ACT, 2015

By
Joy Ngozi Ezeilo,

OON [**Ph.D. (Nig.), LLM (London), LL.B. (Nig.), BL, Diploma Peace & Conflict Res (Uppsala)**]

Abstract

This paper provides an overview of gender-based violence in Nigeria and discusses the making of the milestone federal legislation on Violence Against Persons Prohibition Act (otherwise called the VAPP Act, 2015) from the standpoint of one who was involved in the legislative and social advocacy leading to the adoption of that law. It examines in detail the provisions of the Act, the offences created and punishable thereunder, and importantly, the protection and comprehensive succour it affords victims and survivors of sexual and gender-based violence. It spotlights some innovations under the Act such as compensation and medical assistance to victims, expansion of the offence of rape, prescription of the minimum sentence for convicted rape offenders, sex offenders register, the creation of the offence of stalking, and empowering the court to grant protection order. Finally, it calls for effective implementation of the Act to ensure that violence is prevented and effective investigation and prosecution carried out to hold perpetrators accountable whilst victims/survivors in search of justice can have access to justice and obtain remedies as envisaged under the Act.

Paper Outline

1. Introduction and Context to Gender-based Violence in Nigeria
2. Background to the Making of the VAPP Law
3. Overview of the Violence Against Persons (Prohibition) Act, 2015
   - 3.1. Summary of the Act
   - 3.2. Detailed Consideration of Important Provisions of the VAPP Act, 2015
   - 3.3. Part I – Offences
   - 3.4. Part II – Jurisdiction Of The Court
   - 3.5. Part III – Service Providers
   - 3.6. Part IV – Regulatory Body
   - 3.7. Part V – Consequential Amendment
   - 3.8. Part VI – Interpretations
4. Beyond VAPP Act and Ensuring Effective Implementation
5. Conclusion

1. Introduction and Context to Gender-based Violence in Nigeria

Violence against persons results in cumulative breaches of their rights, including right to life and other sexual and reproductive rights. Whereas it is true that violence affects women and men, it unarguably affects women and girls disproportionately. A woman or girl, for example, who is raped would have to worry about unwanted pregnancy, sexually transmitted infections on top of violation of her right to bodily integrity and mental torture, trauma and emotional distress that are all aftermaths of incidence of sexual violence.

The United Nations General Assembly, in the Declaration on the Elimination of Violence Against Women in 1993, defined the term "Violence Against Women" to mean "any act of gender-based violence that results in, or is likely to result in, physical, sexual or psychological harm or suffering to women, including threats of such acts, coercion or arbitrary deprivation of liberty, whether occurring in public or private life". The definition is further echoed and expatiated upon in the Beijing Platform for Action, 1995.[1] The Protocol to the African Charter on the Rights of Women in Africa, otherwise called

[1] Paragraphs 114-118.

Maputo Protocol, 2003, in article 1 (i) defines violence against women to mean "all acts perpetrated against women which cause or could cause them physical, sexual, psychological, and economic harm, including the threat to take such acts; or to undertake the imposition of arbitrary restrictions on or deprivation of fundamental freedoms in private or public life in peace time and during situations of armed conflicts or of war". From all these definitions and descriptions, it could be deduced that violence against women can be broadly categorised into five types: Physical violence; Psychological violence; Sexual violence; Harmful traditional practices; Socio-economic violence.

In Nigeria, common forms of violence include: Rape; Partner/Wife Battery/ Spousal Beatings; Sexual Harassment; Trafficking in women for sexual and domestic labour; Female Genital Mutilation or Female Circumcision; Forced and Child Marriage; Acid Attack; Female body mutilation for ritual purposes; Denial of Inheritance Rights or share from the assets of deceased father or husband; Harmful Widowhood/Mourning Practices; Emotional Abuse; Abandonment of wife or children without means of subsistence; Sexual slavery; and Dedication to shrine etc.

According to a World Bank Study (1993), violence against women adversely affects victims, family members, perpetrators, communities and nations on profound emotional, physical, psychological and economic levels. It accounts for more death and ill health among women aged 14 to 44 worldwide than cancer, obstructed labour, heart disease, respiratory infections, traffic accidents or even war. The aftermath includes feelings of hopelessness, isolation, guilt and depression, or even suicide. It gravely erodes women's autonomy and bodily integrity, even the sense of self-worth as human beings, and the ability to care for themselves and their children. It leads to bruises, cuts, broken bones or limbs, unwanted pregnancies, STIs/HIV/AIDS, permanent disabilities or death among women of reproductive age. It has been stated to account for 5% of healthy years of life lost to women of reproductive age. Victims and survivors may suffer from loss of human potential and wages, resulting in personal and economic hardship with huge impact on overall development.

Responses to incidences of gender-based violence in Nigeria leave much to be desired. For example, there is no comprehensive law of national application for combating violence against women in all its forms. The absence of enabling legal environment means that victims and survivors of violence against women have little or no recourse to justice. While some states, mainly in the southern part of Nigeria (Edo, Ekiti, Bayelsa, Delta, Rivers, Cross River, Imo, Anambra, Enugu, Ebonyi and Oyo) have enacted gender specific laws prohibiting some forms of violence (FGM, Child/Early Marriage, Trafficking, Safe Motherhood and Widow's Rights Protection) a majority of states have taken no action to combat violence against women. Furthermore, the limited application of State laws to specific states of the Federation, and issue legislated upon - for example: early marriage or female circumcision/ female genital mutilation — means that there is no legal protection against other forms of violence.

Governmental support services for re-integration and rehabilitation of victims are virtually non-existent, despite the fact that the Nigerian government has signed and ratified the United Nations Convention on Elimination of All Forms of Discrimination against Women (CEDAW) and the Protocol on African Charter on Women's Rights, including the Convention Against Torture, as well as the UN Convention on Rights of the Child (1989), UN Convention on Persons with Disabilities, among others. On the other hand, very Few NGOs runs shelter and other support services for battered women and victims/survivors of sexual assault (WACOL, Enugu office and Project Alert, Lagos).

Organisations such as WACOL, FIDA, amongst others, provide free legal aid services across the country for women whose rights have been abused. Other mainstream human rights organisations — LEDAP, CLO, HURILAWS — provide similar services for women on a much lower scale throughout the federation of Nigeria.

In 2014, Women Aid Collective (WACOL) established, in collaboration with partners, a specialised Sexual Assault and Referral Centre called Tamar SARC.[2] This is modelled as an international best practice in responding to the needs of victims of sexual violence. The Centre renders, without discrimination, a confidential and high quality medical, counselling and other support services to victims/survivors of sexual violence, especially

---

[2] TAMAR SARC is a joint Initiative of Enugu State Government, Police, DFID/J4A and WACOL. The Center enjoys financial support from the Justice for All, DfiD/British Council.

women and minors, by supporting their recovery and encouraging increased reporting of rape and other sexual assault cases. Tamar SARC, in about one year of its operation, has received over 300 cases of sexual assaults with more than half of that number (174) perpetrated against girls under the age of 18 years. The Centre helps in reporting the incidents to the police with the client's consent, and ensures that each case is well followed up. It also provides shelter for victims of rape and other sexual violence assault cases at the peak of their crisis. In addition, Tamar SARC runs hotlines that offer free counselling, information and support services over the telephone. All of these were made possible by support from Justice for All/DFID and through the model collaboration with the Enugu State Government through its Ministries of Health, Justice, Gender Affairs and Social Development. The Enugu State Police Command has joined in this new initiative and they do referrals and rapidly respond to our calls for investigations and forensic services. There is also a similar service in Lagos called Mirabel Centre located at the General Hospital, Ikeja. Nevertheless, such services are limited and far between and serving very few of the affected who are privileged to be in close proximity to such service providers.

Sexual violence undoubtedly affects women disproportionately. Women and girls experience sexual violence in their homes, communities, schools, workplaces, streets, markets, police stations and hospitals. It is undeniably the most clandestine form of violation of human rights of women and girls; in particular, the right to personal security, liberty and bodily integrity, including sexual and reproductive self-determination.

Adequate and effective remedies are often inaccessible to victims of sexual and gender-based violence, despite the numerous human rights violations they suffered. While the right to an effective remedy is a well-established norm under international law, in reality there remains a wide gap between the law and its implementation vis-à-vis affected persons. In Nigeria, the laws are inadequate to protect, prevent and combat sexual and gender-based violence as well as punish perpetrators appropriately. Women and girls victims, especially of rape and other forms of sexual assaults, are not provided with remedies as a matter of right. They go through a lot in search of justice, becoming in the process doubly victimised, stigmatised and jeopardised. Sometimes they are publicly humiliated even in court by questions and cross-examination and corroboration required to prove rape.

It was in view of the foregoing that concerned persons and organisations articulated and started pushing for a law to protect, initially, women and girls from all forms of gender-based violence. This was later expanded to include all persons, in realisation that violence, especially sexual violence, affects boys as well.

2. Background to the Making of the VAPP LAW

The journey to the making of this law started in 2001, when the then International Human Rights Law Group, that later became Global Rights Washington DC, Nigeria's office, organised, in collaboration with local Nigerian women's groups, a national workshop at the Dayspring, Wuse Zone 6, Abuja on violence against women to deliberate on legislative measures to combat and prevent violence. It was at that meeting that the drafting of the bill began and a committee of four persons was set up to co-ordinate and follow up under the chairperson of Dr. Charmaine Pereira. I was privileged to be part of the initial promoters and drafters of this bill. Also, following therefrom, a network of organisations to champion social and legislative advocacy, known as Legislative Advocacy Coalition on Violence against Women (LACVAW), was born with the singular mandate to pursue legislative and social advocacy towards the enactment of comprehensive law to combat and prevent gender-based violence.

LACVAW, co-ordinated at first by WRAPA under the leadership of Hajiya Saudatu Mahdi and later on by FIDA, with Hauwa Shekarau at the helm, was very instrumental in leading advocacy and mobilising civil society, in particular women's groups, media and the international community to support advocacy towards its enactment. It is also pertinent to mention that in 2005, the then Attorney General and Minister of Justice, Chief Bayo Ojo (SAN), set up a Committee to draft a bill on Elimination of Violence in Society. I was appointed to chair this committee that produced a draft bill brought to the National Assembly as an Executive Bill, and which was sponsored by Senator Victor Ndoma-Egba. It was later harmonised alongside other bills prohibiting gender-based violence that transformed to what became known as the VAPP bill by 2009. Since 2002, the VAPP bill failed to get passed through the life time of successive legislative chambers of both houses of the National Assembly.

It was not until the 7th Assembly that we started to record milestones. At the commencement of the 7th National Assembly (2011-2015), the Bill was re-introduced and sponsored by Hon. Abike Dabiri-Erewa and finally got passed by the House of Representatives on March 14, 2013. Thereafter, it was transmitted to the Senate in April of 2013. With that the struggle moved to the Senate for concurrence to the "Violence against Persons (Prohibition) Bill". The bill passed first and second readings by March 18 and October 16 2014 respectively and was consequently referred to the Senate Committee on Judiciary, Human Rights and Legal Matters. The bill was sponsored by then Senate leader, Senator Victor Ndoma-Egba (SAN), and the Committee on Judiciary, Human Rights and Legal Matters, under the leadership of Senator Dahiru Umar, played a key role leading to its final passage. The Committee organised a public hearing on March 2, 2015[3] and between March and April 2015, the bill was considered by the Senate and some areas of contention resolved with the active involvement of LACVAW. The VAPP bill got the final nod and was passed on 5th May, 2015 by the senate.

The public hearing was highly instrumental in the final push that the time has come to do the right thing by legislating against gender-based violence. Women's groups and their supporters, including Muslim clerics came out in their numbers to urge for its passage. Also, worthy of note is the enormous support it got from international organisations such as DfID/J4A, Ipas, Voice for Change/UK Aid, UNODC, among others. Ipas, for example, through its work with LACVAW, Medical Women, FOMWAN, and WACOL, successfully made the VAPP bill agenda a front burner national issue. Ipas co-ordinated and supported the participation of over 600 women and men at the Public Hearing on the VAPP bill organised by the Senate on March 2, 2015.

WACOL, as a foundation member of the Legislative Advocacy Network on Violence against Women (LACVAW), has been involved since inception, especially through the contributions of its founding director, Joy Ngozi Ezeilo, in the drafting and follow up social and legislative advocacy towards the passage of the law on violence against persons. At the Public

[3] The public hearing was very well attended and the voice of Nigerian women clamouring for the passage of the bill was heard loud and clear. See newspaper reports: DAILY INDEPENDENT- "Nigerian women and passage of bill on violence" by Yinka Shokunbi, March 10, 2014; VANGUARD March 10, "Agitations Heightens for Passage of VAPP Bill" p. 36.

Hearing organised by the Senate on March 2, 2015, WACOL submitted a comprehensive memorandum to the Senate Committee on Judiciary, Human Rights and Legal Matters making a strong case for the immediate passage of the law, including suggestions for its expansion to include, for example, a register of sexual offenders, criminalise sexual harassment; and to also provide for comprehensive health care for victims of violence. Prior to that, on October 23, 2014, WACOL organised a Mock Tribunal/Court on Sexual and Gender-based Violence right inside the parliament in collaboration with the National Assembly Women Affairs Committee and Ipas. The Mock Tribunal/Court was used to spotlight cases of gender-based violence in Nigeria and raise the voices of victims and survivors towards urgent action in enacting protective laws, especially the passage into law of the Violence against Persons Prohibition Bill.[4]

On May 25, 2015, the immediate past President of Nigeria, Goodluck Ebele Jonathan, recorded a milestone when he signed into Law the Violence Against Persons Prohibition Act, 2015. This brought to a successful conclusion the 13-year long social and legislative advocacy championed by women's groups and gender activists towards the passage of this law that will protect persons, especially women and girls, from all forms of violence.

3. Overview of the Violence Against Persons (Prohibition) Act, 2015

3.1. Summary of the Act

This Act, according to its long title, is aimed at eliminating violence in private and public life; prohibiting all forms of violence, including physical, sexual, psychological, domestic, harmful traditional practices; halting discrimination against persons to providing maximum protection and effective remedies for victims and punishment of offenders. It has a total of 48 sections divided into six main parts: Offences; Jurisdiction of the Court; Service Providers; Regulatory Body, Consequential Amendment, and Interpretations.

This Act commendably covers most of the prevalent forms of violence that could be categorised into: Physical violence; Psychological violence;

---

[4] See THISDAY Newspaper report on the Mock tribunal October 24, 2014 titled "Rape Victims Besiege N'Assembly, Seek Passage of Sexual Offences Bill" and written by Omololu Ogunmade.

Sexual violence; Harmful traditional practices; Socio-economic violence. Specifically, The VAPP Act comprehensively dealt with one of the most vexing forms of sexual violence — rape — which under existing penal laws protects only females and is limited to vaginal penetration. It has expanded the scope of rape to protect males and to include anal and oral sex as well as protect the identity of rape victims. The following are offences punishable under the Act: Rape; Inflicting Physical Injury on a Person; Female Circumcision or Genital Mutilation; Forceful Ejection from Home; Depriving a Person of His / Her Liberty; Forced Financial Dependence or Economic Abuse; Forced Isolation or Separation from Family and Friends; Emotional Verbal and Psychological Abuse; Harmful Widowhood Practices; Abandonment of Spouse, Children and Other Dependant without Sustenance; Spousal/ Partner Battery; Indecent exposure; Harmful Traditional Practices; Political Violence; and Violence by State Actors. Other innovations in this Act include the prohibition and punishment for stalking, substance attack, criminalising incestuous conducts, protection order for victims and persons under threat of violence, and compensation for victims of violence. It provided for a register for convicted sexual offenders, which shall be maintained and accessible to the public.

Importantly, the Act contained provisions on effective remedies, including the rights of victims to assistance. According to section 38 "Every victim is entitled to receive the necessary materials, comprehensive medical, psychological, social and legal assistance through governmental agencies and/or non-governmental agencies providing such assistance". Victims are entitled to be informed of the availability of legal, health and social services and other relevant assistance and be readily afforded access to them. Furthermore, it provides that: "Victims are entitled to rehabilitation and re-integration programme of the State to enable victims to acquire, where applicable and necessary, pre-requisite skills in any vocation of the victim's choice and also in necessary formal education or access to micro credit facilities".

3.2. Detailed Consideration of Important Provisions of the VAPP Act, 2015

The methodology will be to examine in detail some provisions considered important and to compartmentalise them according to the six main parts of the VAPP Act. Before embarking on a discussion of these specific provisions in different parts of the law, I would like to highlight, first, some general definitions that go to the fundamental objective of this law as one that is aimed at prohibiting violence in private and public spheres. It is welcome that this Act has a section that comprehensively defined keywords and terms of importance to the law. While I will not refer to all in one fell swoop, the following, outlined below, are of preliminary and broad importance to understanding the context of this Act and the implications of offences created, criminalised and punished. The definitions of keywords to aid understanding of offences prohibited and punished are alphabetically arranged in s. 46. However, it should be observed that my mention of them did not necessarily follow that pattern but rather on consideration of their relevance to the issue at hand for discussion.

Highlights of some definitions provided by the VAPP ACT, 2015

"Violence" in this Act, unless the context otherwise requires, means any act or attempted act, which causes or may cause any person physical, sexual, psychological, verbal, emotional or economic harm whether this occurs in private or public life, in peace time and in conflict situations;

"Domestic Violence" means any act perpetrated on any person in a domestic relationship where such act causes harm or may cause imminent harm to the safety, health or well-being of any person;

"Physical abuse" means acts or threatened acts of physical aggression towards any person such as slapping, hitting kicking and beating;

"Economic abuse" means forced financial dependence; denial of inheritance or succession rights, the unreasonable deprivation of economic or financial resources to which any person is entitled or which any person requires out of necessity, including household necessities, mortgage bond repayments or payment of rent in respect of a shared residence; the unreasonable disposal or destruction of household effects or other property in which any person has an interest;

"Harassment" means engaging in a pattern of conduct that induces fear of harm or impairs the dignity of a person including stalking; repeatedly making telephone calls or inducing another person to make telephone calls to a person, whether or not conversation ensues; repeatedly sending, delivering or causing delivery of information such as letters, telegrams, packages, facsimiles, electronic mail, text messages or other objects to any person;

"Violence in the private sphere" means any act or attempted act perpetrated by a member of the family, relative, neighbour or member of a community, which causes or may cause any person physical, sexual, psychological, verbal, emotional or economic harm;

"Violence in the public sphere" means any act or attempted act perpetrated by the State or non-State actors before, during and after elections, in conflict or war situations, which threatens peace, security and well-being of any person or the nation as a whole;

"Violence perpetrated by non-state actors" includes:

(i) wrongful arrest and detention;
(ii) assault;
(iii) use of force without lawful authority;
(iv) unlawful entry into the premises;
(v) demolition of property without due processes;

"Victim" means any person or persons, who, individually or collectively, have suffered harm, including physical or mental injury, emotional suffering, economic loss or substantial impairment of their fundamental rights, through acts or omissions that are in violation of this Bill and/or the criminal laws of the country. Victim also includes the immediate family or dependents of the direct victim and any other person who has suffered harm in intervening to assist victims in distress; and

"Perpetrator" means any person who has committed or allegedly committed an act of violence as defined above.

"Vulnerable groups" means women, children, persons living under extreme poverty, persons with disability, the sick and the elderly, ethnic and religious minority groups, refugees, internally displaced persons, migrants and persons in detention.

3.3. PART I - OFFENCES

This part is broken into twenty six (26) sections. The part started with section 1 and ended with section 26 of the Act. The sections contain different and various offences on violence against persons. The offences are centred on preventing and prohibiting violence against persons. Also, the offences made provision for penalty or payment of fines or both penalties and fines. Offences criminalised and sanctioned include: rape, incest, indecent exposure, female circumcision or general mutilation, forceful ejection from home, depriving a person of his or her liberty, forced financial dependence or economic abuse, forced isolation or separation from family and friends, emotional, verbal and psychological abuse. Others are: harmful widowhood practices, abandonment of spouse, children and other dependents without sustenance, stalking, intimidation, spousal battery, harmful traditional practices, attack with harmful substances, including administering a substance with the intention of stupefying or overpowering that person so as to enable any person to engage in a sexual activity with that person.

(a) On Rape: Section 1 defines rape and according to that section (1) Rape offence occurs where a person intentionally penetrates the vagina, anus, or mouth of another person with other part of his body or anything else without consent or where consent is obtained the consent, is obtained by force or means of threat or intimidation of any kind or by fear of harm or by means of false and fraudulent representation as to the nature of the act or the use of any substance or addictive capable of taking away the will of such person or in the case of a married person by impersonating his/her spouse/partner. The penalty is imprisonment for life and a maximum of 14 years imprisonment for offender less than 14 years[5]; and a minimum of 12 years imprisonment without option of fine in other cases.[6] In relation to gang rape the punishment is a minimum of 20 years imprisonment for each person in the case of rape by a group of persons.[7] There is a provision empowering the court to award appropriate compensation

---

[5] S. 1 (2) (a).

[6] S. 1 (2) (b).

[7] S. 1(2) (C).

to victims of rape.[8] Section 1 (4) provides for a register for convicted sexual offenders which shall be maintained and accessible to the public.

(b) On Incest: This means an indecent act or an act which causes penetration with a person who is to his/her knowledge his/her daughter/son, granddaughter/son, sister/brother, mother/father, niece/nephew, aunt/uncle, grandmother/granduncle.[9] Section 25 prohibits incestuous relationships and makes it an offence to knowingly and willfully having carnal knowledge of another within the prohibited degree of consanguinity. This offence is punishable with 10 years imprisonment without an option of fine. It should be observed that consent to commit the offence of incest by two parties without fraud or threat is still an offence and the punishment is five years imprisonment without an option of fine.

(c) On Indecent Exposure, s. 26 (1) stipulates that any person who intentionally exposes his or her genital organs, or a substantial part thereof, with the intention of causing distress to the other party, or that another person seeing it may be tempted or induced to commit an offence under this Act, commits an offence. Further termed indecent exposure is a situation where any person intentionally exposes his or her genital organs, or a substantial part thereof, and induces another to either massage, or touch with the intention of deriving sexual pleasure from such acts.[10] The penalty for any intentional exposure of one's genital organ is one year imprisonment or fine of N500,000 or both. "Indecent exposure" is defined in the act as the intentional exposure of the genital organs, or a substantial part thereof, with the intention of causing distress to the other party.

(d) Administering a substance with intent — s. 22: Any person who administers or causes a substance to be administered to a person with the intention of stupefying or overpowering that person so as to enable any person to engage in a sexual activity with that person

8 Section 1 (3).

9 S. 46.

10 See s. 26 (2).

commits an offence under this Act. The punishment provided is 10 years imprisonment or fine of N500,000 or both.

(e) Offensive conduct: section 5. (1) provides that any person who compels another by force or threat to engage in any conduct or act sexual or otherwise, to the detriment of the victim's physical or psychological well-being commits an offence and is liable on conviction to imprisonment for a term not exceeding two years or to fine not exceeding N500,000 or to both such fine and imprisonment.[11]

I would like to briefly highlight some provisions with implication for sexual crimes already discussed above, to enhance our understanding of areas previously unknown in our penal system. These definitions cover: sexual abuse, sexual assault, sexual exploitation, sexual harassment and sexual intimidation. According to section 46 on interpretation:

"Sexual abuse" means any conduct, which violates, humiliates or degrades the sexual integrity of any person;

"Sexual assault" means the intentional and unlawful touching, striking or causing of bodily harm to an individual in a sexual manner without his/her consent;

"Sexual exploitation" occurs where a perpetrator, for financial or other reward, favour or compensation invites, persuades, engages or induces the services of a victim, or offers or performs such services to any other person;

"Sexual harassment" means unwanted conduct of a sexual nature or other conduct based on sex or gender which is persistent or serious and demeans, humiliates or creates a hostile or intimidating environment. This may include physical, verbal or non-verbal conduct;

Sexual intimidation means:

(a) any action or circumstances which amount to demand for sexual intercourse with either a male or a female under any guise, as a condition

[11] Note that attempts to commit the offence provided for in subsection (1) attracts 1 year imprisonment or a fine of N300,000.00 or both.

for passing examination, securing employment, business patronage, obtaining any favour in any form whatsoever, as may be defined in this Act or any other enactments;

(b) the actual demand for sexual intercourse with either a male or female under any guise, as a condition for passing examination, securing employment, business patronage and or obtaining any favour in any form whatsoever, as may be defined in this Act or any other enactments;

(c) acts of deprivation, withholding, replacing and or short-changing of entitlements, privileges, rights, benefits, examination or test marks/ scores, and any other form of disposition capable of coercing any person to submit to sexual intercourse for the purpose of receiving reprieve thereto;

(d) any other action or inaction construed as sexual intimidation/harassment under any other enactments in force in Nigeria.

These definitions will no doubt guide the courts in the application and interpretation of the VAPP Act.

(f) Prohibition of female circumcision or genital mutilation is covered in section 6. Thus, a person who performs female circumcision or genital mutilation or engages another in the act of female circumcision or genital mutilation commits an offence and the sanction is four years imprisonment (maximum) or fine of N200,000 (maximum). In the same vein, it punishes any person who aids and abets or attempts to commit the offence and under subsection (1) of this section, the person commits an offence for which the penalty will not exceed two years imprisonment or a fine of N100,000 or both.[12] In this Act "Circumcision of a girl or woman" means cutting off all or part of the external sex organs of a girl or woman other than on medical ground.[13]

(g) Forced isolation or separation from family and friends: Any person who forcefully isolates or separates another from family

[12] See s. 6 (3) and (4).

[13] S. 46.

and friends commits an offence and is liable on conviction to imprisonment for a term not exceeding six months or to fine not exceeding N100,000 or to both such fine and imprisonment. Attempted forced isolation or separation from family and friends as well as aiding and abetting commission of such offence is similarly sanctioned.[14] It should be observed from the definition in section 44 that "Forced isolation from family and friends" includes, but is not limited to, preventing a person from leaving the home or from having contact with family, friends or the outside community.

(h) Emotional verbal and psychological abuse is criminalised by s. 14. Consequently, any person who causes emotional, verbal and psychological abuse on another commits an offence and is liable on conviction to imprisonment for a term not exceeding one year or to fine not exceeding N200,000 or to both such fine and imprisonment.[15] In this Act, "Emotional, verbal and psychological abuse" means a pattern of degrading or humiliating conduct towards any person, including repeated insults, ridicule or name calling; repeated threats to cause emotional pain; or the repeated exhibition of obsessive possessiveness, which is of such a nature as to constitute a serious invasion of such person's privacy, liberty, integrity or security.

(i) Harmful widowhood practices are prohibited as a form of violence against person in s. 15 (1); and any person who subjects a widow to harmful traditional practices commits an offence and is liable on conviction to imprisonment for a term not exceeding two years or to fine not exceeding N500,000 or to both such fine and imprisonment. A person who incites, aids, abets, or counsels another person to commit widowhood practices is guilty of an offence and is liable on

---

[14] S. 13 (2) & (3). By s. 13 (4), a person who receives or assists another who to his or her knowledge committed the offence under subsection (1) of this section commits an offence that will be penalised by three months imprisonment or fine of N100,000 or both.

[15] Attempting to commit emotional, verbal and psychological abuse, including inciting, aiding, abetting, receiving or assisting are all prohibited and punished on conviction to a term not exceeding six months or to a fine not exceeding N100,000 or both.

conviction to imprisonment for a term not exceeding one year or to fine not exceeding N200,000 or to both such fine and imprisonment.[16] It is pertinent to note the definition of "Harmful traditional practices", which means all traditional behaviour, attitudes and/or practices, which negatively affect the fundamental rights of women, girls, or any person and includes harmful widowhood practices, denial of inheritance or succession rights, female genital mutilation or female circumcision, forced marriage and forced isolation from family and friends.[17]

(j) Harmful traditional practices: A person who carries out harmful traditional practices on another as defined above commits an offence for which he or she would be punished with imprisonment for a term of four years or fine of N500,000 or both.[18]

(k) Stalking: means repeatedly watching, or loitering outside of or near the building or place where such person resides, works, carries on business, studies or happens to be; or repeatedly following, pursuing or accosting any person in a manner which induces fear or anxiety.[19] Any person who stalks another commits an offence and is liable on conviction to imprisonment for a term not exceeding two years or to fine not exceeding N500,000 or to both such fine and imprisonment.[20]

(l) "Intimidation" means according to s. 46 on interpretation “the uttering or conveying of a threat or causing any person to receive a threat, which induces fear, anxiety or discomfort. "Spousal / Partner battery" means the intentional and unlawful use of force or violence upon a person, including the unlawful touching, beating or striking

---

16 Note that attempt to commit such offence prohibited in s. 15 (1) is similarly punished while accessory after the fact is punished with imprisonment to a term not exceeding one year or to a fine not exceeding N200,000 or both- s.15 (4).

17 S. 46.

18 S. 20.

19 S. 46.

20 See s. 17. Also attempted stalking is punished for a maximum term of one year imprisonment or a fine of N200, 000 or both. A person who incites, aids, abets or counsels another to commit the act of violence in respect of stalking is also guilty- see s. 17 (2) and (3).

of another person against his/her will with the intention of causing bodily harm to that person". Intimidation of a person is penalised by section 18 and liability on conviction to imprisonment for a term not exceeding one year or to fine not exceeding N200,000 or to both such fine and imprisonment.[21]

(m) Spousal/Partner battery: According to s. 19 any person who batters his or her spouse commits offence of which the penalty is one year imprisonment for intimidation and three years imprisonment for spouse battering or fine of N200,000 (maximum) or both. Equally, any attempt to commit or incite one to commit the offence under sub-section (1) of this section is an offence.[22] "Spousal/ Partner battery" means the intentional and unlawful use of force or violence upon a person, including the unlawful touching, beating or striking of another person against his/her will with the intention of causing bodily harm to that person.

(n) Attack with harmful substance is prohibited by s. 21 and heavily punished. The section provides that any person who uses chemical, biological or any other harmful liquid on another person commits an offence. The penalty is life imprisonment without option of fine. Also, an attempt to commit or incite the committing of offence under subsection (1) of this section is an offence and the penalty, including for an accessory is 25 years without an option of fine.[23] "Substance attack" means the exposure of any person to any form of chemical, biological or any other harmful liquid with the intention to cause grievous bodily harm, which includes but is not limited to acid attack, hot water, hot oil.[24]

(o) Forceful ejection from home: section 9 stipulates that: any marriage partner who forcefully evicts his/her partner from his/her home or refuses him/her access commits an offence and is liable on conviction

---

21 See s. 18 (1-4).

22 A Penalty of one year imprisonment or Fine of N100, 000 or both will be visited on the offender upon conviction.

23 See also s. 20 (2)- (4).

24 S. 46.

to imprisonment for a term not exceeding two years or to fine not exceeding N300,000 or to both such fine and imprisonment. Any person who aids, abets, attempts to commit violence or receives or assists another knowing him to have committed violence is liable to imprisonment not exceeding one year of a fine of not exceeding N200,000.[25]

(p) Forced financial dependence or economic abuse: By s. 12. (1) – "Any person who causes forced financial dependence or economic abuse of another commits an offence and is liable on conviction to imprisonment for a term not exceeding two years or to fine not exceeding N500,000 or to both such fine and imprisonment."

(q) Abandonment of spouse, children and other dependants without sustenance has been criminalised by s. 16 and the punishment on conviction is imprisonment for a term not exceeding three years or to fine not exceeding N500,000 or to both such fine and imprisonment.[26] "Abandonment of women, children and other persons" means deliberately leaving women, children and other persons under the perpetrator's care, destitute and without any means of subsistence.[27]

(r) Political violence: section 23 (1) provides that any person who commits political violence as defined in this Act commits an offence and is liable on conviction to imprisonment for four years or fine of N500,000 or both. Any state actor who commits political violence is liable to the same punishment.[28] "Political violence" is defined in this Act to mean any act or attempted act of violence perpetrated in the course of political activities, such as elections, and includes any of the following acts: thuggery, mugging, use of force to disrupt

---

25 S. 9 (2)-(4).

26 By s. 16 (2) and (3) attempting to commit or inciting, aiding, abetting another person to commit violence under subsection (1) of this section is an offence. Penalty: two years imprisonment or fine: N200,000 or both. Also s. 16 (4) stipulates that receiving or assisting any person knowing that the person committed the violence under subsection (1) of this section is an offence. Penalty: six months imprisonment or fine: N100,000 or both.

27 S. 46.

28 See s. 24 (1).

meetings, or the use of dangerous weapons that may cause bodily harm or injury.[29]

3.4. PART II – JURISDICTION OF THE COURT

Part II covered sections 27 to 38. The sections under this part dealt with issues of jurisdiction of the court[30], application for, consideration and issuance of protection order[31]. Application for protection order may be made before the High Court by a complaint of violence by the complainant or through his or her counsel or any other person such as the Police protection officer, accredited service providers, a counselor, health service provider, social worker or teacher who has interest in the well-being of the complainant.[32]

All applications for protection order shall be with the consent of the complainant except in the following circumstances where the complainant is:

(a) a minor,
(b) mentally retarded,
(c) unconscious, or
(d) a person unable to give consent satisfactory to the court.

The Court has enormous powers as to order(s) it can make while issuing protection order in favour of the complainant against a respondent. These may include obligations on respondent to pay rent, mortgage, secure alternative accommodation for the complainant, and pay emergency monetary relief having regard to the financial needs and resources of the complainant and the respondent.[33]

---

[29] See s. 46 on Interpretation.

[30] See s. 27.

[31] See sections 28-29.

[32] See s. 28 (3) to (4). S. 30 and 31 contains court powers and conditions for issuing of a protection order. By s. 31 (2) – the Court may impose any additional condition, which it deems reasonably necessary to protect and provide for the safety, health or well- being of the complainant, including an order to seize any arm or dangerous weapon in the possession or under the control of the respondent. The court can also direct a police officer to accompany the complainant to a specified place to assist with arrangements regarding the collection of personal property-s. 31 (2) (b); and it can direct the respondent o secure alternative accommodation for the complainant.

[33] S. 31 subsections 2 to 8.

Other issues considered under this part are: powers of police[34], warrant of arrest[35], offences relating to protection order and rights of victims of violent acts to remedies, including comprehensive medical assistance, shelter and psycho-social support. Section 38 extensively covered rights of victims and expressly states that rights recognised in this section should be accorded to every victim of violence in addition to the rights guaranteed under Chapter IV of the Constitution of the Federal Republic of Nigeria, 1999, or any other international human rights instrument to which Nigeria is a party.[36] The rights of victims recognised are as follows:

(a) To receive the necessary materials, comprehensive medical, psychological, social and legal assistance from governmental or non-governmental agencies
(b) To be informed of availability of legal, health and social services
(c) To rehabilitation and reintegration programme through skill acquisition in any vocation of victim's choice, formal education or access to micro-credit facilities

The section further provides that rules and or regulation prohibiting or restraining the reporting of the offence of violence is null and void and of no effect; and that no complainant shall be punished for compliance with provisions of the Act.[37]

3.5. PART III – SERVICE PROVIDERS

Part III of the Act dealt with the issue of service providers. There are about five sections of the part beginning with section 39 and ending with section

---

[34] S. 32. The powers of police are extensive and includes: assisting a victim of violence to file a complaint regarding the violence, providing a safe transportation, safe place or shelter, explaining to the victim his or her rights to protection against violence and remedies available in terms of this Act, explaining to the victim that he or she has the right to lodge a criminal complaint in addition to any remedy provided under this Act; and accompanying the victim to victim's residence to collect personal belongings.

[35] A police officer may, without an order from the Court or a warrant of arrest, arrest any person whom he or she suspects upon reasonable grounds to have committed any of the offences under part 1 of this Act; and a complaint has been made for having committed any of the offences under Part 1 of this Act.

[36] See s. 38 (1).

[37] Ibid. subsection 38 (1) d and e.

43. Section 39 dealt with the issue of prohibition of publication of certain information concerning the identity of victims and persons involved in court proceedings for a protection order. This is an important provision to ensure right to privacy and confidentiality given the intra-familial nature of cases that may be brought under this law and likely effect on family, especially the children. Any person who contravenes the provisions of this sub-section is guilty of an offence and is liable upon conviction to imprisonment for a term not exceeding one year or to fine not exceeding N200,000 or to both such fine and imprisonment.[38] Section 40 considered registration and powers of service providers. According to s. 40:

> Subject to such rules as may be made, any voluntary association registered under the Companies and Allied Matters Act 1990 by the Corporate Affairs Commission or any other law for the time being in force with the objective of protecting the rights and interests of victims of violence by any lawful means including providing of legal aid, medical, financial or other assistance shall register itself with the State Government as a service provider for the purposes of this Act.[39]

A registered service provider shall have powers to: (a) record the violent incident report in the prescribed form if the aggrieved person so desires and forward a copy thereof to the Magistrates and the Protection Officer having jurisdiction in the area where the violence took place; (b) get the aggrieved person medically examined and forward a copy of the medical report to the Protection Officer and the Police station within the locality of which the violence act took place; and (c) ensure that the aggrieved person is provided shelter in a shelter home, if she so requires and forward a report of the lodging of the aggrieved person in the shelter home to the police station within the locality of which the violence act took place.[40] A service provider acting in good faith is granted immunity and protected from prosecution or any legal proceedings arising in the course of the exercise of their powers under

---

[38] S. 39 (3).

[39] An appropriate Government Ministry shall be required to keep a register of all accredited service providers and circulate same to all police stations, protection officers and the courts; and draw up guidelines for the operation of the accredited service providers. See s. 40 (2) (a) and (b).

[40] Section 40 (3) a-c.

this Act, including service providers' action towards the prevention of the commission of violence.[41]

Section 41 dealt with the issue of appointment of protection officers in Area Councils and their functions – which primarily focused on assisting the court in discharge of its duties under the law, co-ordination of the activities of the police and accredited service providers in his Area Council and ensuring that victims of violence have:

(a) easy access to accredited service provider.
(b) easy access to transportation to alternative residence or a safe shelter, hospital, etc.
(c) are able to access the court for orders under this Act; and
(d) access to assistance for service of interim protection order on the respondent and the enforcement thereof

Finally, sections 42 and 43 of the Act considered appointment of co-ordinator for prevention of domestic violence, and declaration of dangerous sexual offender. The coordinator will be appointed by the body vested with the regulation of this Act (i.e. NAPTIP) and the co-ordinator shall submit annual report to the Federal Government on the implementation of this Act. A copy of this report would be deposited with the National Bureau for Statistics.

a) Section 43 is an important addition to this Act and dealt with dangerous sexual offenders. A court may declare a person who has been convicted of a sexual offence a dangerous sexual offender if such person has: (a) more than one conviction for a sexual offence; (b) been convicted of a sexual offence which was accompanied with grievous harm or threat to life of the victim and (c) been convicted of a sexual offence against a child.

3.6. PART IV – REGULATORY BODY

This topic is handled specifically under section 44 of the Act. Under this section, the regulatory body of the Act was appointed and it is NAPTIP which

---

[41] S. 40 (4).

stands for National Agency for the Prohibition of Trafficking in Persons and other related matters. The body's mandates are:

(a) Administering the provisions of the Act; and
(b) Collaborating with relevant stakeholders, including faith-based organisation

3.7. PART V – CONSEQUENTIAL AMENDMENT

Under this part, there is only one section and it is section 45 of the Act. The section dealt with provisions concerning General savings and repeal. Section 45 (1) allowed and permitted offences committed under such existing laws like the Criminal Code, Penal Code and the Criminal Procedure Code which said offences are similar to the provisions provided under the Act to continue to be enforced. Section 45 (2) took charge of the repeal clause and provided for the provisions of the Act to supersede similar provisions in the Criminal Code, Penal Code and the Criminal Procedure Code.

3.8. PART VI – INTERPRETATIONS

This part is the concluding part and there are three sections therein. The said sections are sections 46, 47 and 48. Section 46 dealt with interpretation or definition of words, terms and unique expressions in the Act. Section 47 treated the issue of Application. The Act applies or is applicable at the Federal Capital Territory Abuja. Section 48, the concluding section handled the issue of citation which of course is the identity of the law and gave the law its name and title. It provides that this Act may be cited as the Violence Against Persons (Prohibition) Act, 2015.

4. Beyond VAPP Act and Ensuring Effective Implementation

There is a comprehensive law now applicable to at least the Federal Capital Territory to combat and prevent gender-based violence. The challenge now is to shift focus from standard setting to implementation of the VAPP Act. Most often interest wanes once a law is passed and civil society, basking in the euphoria of mission accomplished by enactment of such laws, tend to relax and move to other things, including advocacy for more laws with little thought and/or strategy on how to ensure effective and efficacious implementation of extant laws. Undoubtedly, the VAPP Act introduced a number of innovations hitherto unknown in Nigeria's criminal justice system thereby making it very demanding, especially in terms of human and financial resources required to effectively implement this law.

The first step is to sensitise stakeholders about this law, build capacity of administrators of justice, including the police, prosecutors, judges, and other court personnel. The process of applying and obtaining protection order will require special training and sensitisation programmes for both lawyers and service providers who will from time to time represent complainants filing for protection order.

Importantly, the target group for which this law is intended to protect should be sensitised to recognise their rights and to respond appropriately when their rights are violated by seeking for redress and assistance provided under the VAPP Act.

The key ministries need to understand their responsibilities under this law and take immediate action to comply with its provisions. The Act, for example, requires a register of convicted offenders to be maintained. It is not clear whose responsibility this should be whether it is the Police, the Federal Ministry of Justice or a department in FCT bureaucracy or Federal High Court or FCT, High Court as the case may be. Of course one may argue that the implementing agency — NAPTIP should keep such register. However, we must not forget that NAPTIP has its primary responsibility of combating human trafficking and related offences and is under-resourced to tackle their huge mandate. This added burden by VAPP Act would require additional resources to execute. There is a provision in s. 32 (3) (c) that mandates a police officer in carrying out his or her duties under this Act to collect and store fingerprints, including DNA of accused and convicted offenders. This may take a while to implement because of lack of adequate infrastructure and capacity by police to gather such forensic evidence. I think what is needed is continuing education and improvement in infrastructure as well as adequate funding by the Federal Government or FCT in order for this law to achieve its laudable objectives.

5. Conclusion

This Violence Against Persons (Prohibition) Act, long overdue in coming, will unarguably bring succor and effective remedies to millions of victims who have suffered in silence without recourse to justice or rehabilitative and psycho-social support for their recovery and reintegration.

The Act recognised that the treatment and support for physical and emotional injury for victims and survivors would require comprehensive medical assistance, including counseling and appropriate shelter or safe place at the peak of crisis. The Act affords access and better services for victims/survivors of violence, such as hotlines, shelters, legal advice, access to justice, counselling, police protection, and comprehensive health services. The only drawback in relation to this law is its limited application to the Federal Capital Territory, Abuja. This is as a result of the nature of Nigeria's federal structure and constitutional distribution of powers between the Federal Government and States of the Federation. It is expected that the 36 states of Nigeria will take immediate and necessary action to adopt and enact similar law on violence against persons.

COMPARATIVE ANALYSIS OF THE VIOLENCE AGAINST PERSONS (PROHIBITION) ACT (2015) AND THE ENUGU STATE VIOLENCE AGAINST PERSONS PROHIBITION LAW, 2019

By
Uchechukwu Nwoke

Abstract

The phenomenon of violence is pervasive in contemporary societies. The elimination of such violence (especially the ones that are gender-based) has been increasingly recognised as a priority for the international community. Nigeria has joined the bandwagon by enacting the Violence Against Persons (Prohibition) Act (2015), a federal legislation. Many States have also domesticated the legislation in their areas of jurisdiction. Enugu State is one of such States. This paper, while undertaking a comparative analysis of the Violence Against Persons (Prohibition Act (2015) and the Enugu State Violence Against Persons Prohibition Law, 2019, seeks to sensitise the police on existing laws on violence, especially against women and girls and strengthen the capacity of the police to provide effective responses to victims of violence. The paper adopts the doctrinal methodology.

Introduction

In Nigeria, a large number of persons, especially women, are regularly subjected to violence, both in the family and the communities. This situation is exacerbated by the intensely patriarchal societies that encourage men to view women as subordinate and inferior beings. This situation promotes male sexuality and power associated with masculinity. Discriminatory laws condone and even legalise certain forms of violence against persons (especially women). The police and the criminal justice system have not satisfactorily offered protection to victims of violence by dismissing the seriousness of such violence which they consider to be a private or family matter; only reluctantly intervening where absolutely unavoidable.[42] The inability of law enforcement officers (especially the police) to adequately respond to and investigate cases of violence (especially against women) and to prosecute suspected perpetrators is a major obstacle to addressing the issue of violence.

Administration of justice (particularly law enforcement) represents the entry point to the criminal justice system for a substantial number of victims. In this context, the Police are often the first members of the law enforcement machinery encountered by victims of gender-based violence. A proactive and aggressive police response can, therefore, deter further violence and ultimately save lives. Diligent and proactive law enforcement intervention can increase victim safety, enhance investigations and facilitate successful prosecution. It is critical to train administrators of justice to respond effectively to cases of violence against women while being sensitive to the vulnerabilities of victims.

While undertaking a comparative analysis of the Violence against Persons (prohibition Act (2015) and the Enugu State Violence Against Persons Prohibition Law, 2019, this paper seeks to sensitise the police on existing laws on violence, especially against women and girls, strengthen the capacity of the police to provide effective responses to victims of violence and finally to improve police enforcement of relevant laws on violence (especially against women and girls).

Origin of Violence

Violence is present in the very structure of the universe.[43] Perhaps, there has been no age or civilisation without violence. Man is a social being and

---

[42] *Nigeria Unheard Voices – Violence against Women in the Family* (Amnesty International; Stop Violence against Women, 2005)1; see also Joy Ezeilo and Onyinye Ohia (2006): *Torture and The Female Gender – Report of A National Survey on Torture in Nigeria* (Women's Aid Collective (WACOL), 2006).

[43] KM Butt and K Shareef, 'Violence in Historical Perspective' (2013) 31 The Journal of Political Science, 69

for his multiple needs, he has to interact with his fellow beings. He is also power hungry. Since ages, man is passing through an evolutionary process and is facing violence. Genocide, wars, murder, battle, inter-state conflicts, beheading, amputation, blinding, and tribal feuds, all were outcome of evolutionary process. Some of the religious rituals were incomplete without human sacrifices and violent punishments. History is full of violent savagery and barbarism.[44]

The origins of violent and aggressive behaviour have been studied for many years by a great number of researchers from many disciplines: psychology, medicine, sociology, anthropology, ethology, biology, ecology, law, education, and other sciences.[45] Disturbed by the prevalence of violence in contemporary societies, parents, legislators, criminologists, policemen, theologians, psychologists, teachers, politicians and health care providers are all alarmed and looking for some deeper understanding that might lead to practical steps to deal with the problem. The result of this feverish activity is a massive and multiplying literature measured in thousands of articles, books, conferences and media productions. Nevertheless, in all this activity the origin of violence is very rarely explored.[46] According to Sorrel, 2 per cent of human deaths are caused by human(s) via violence.[47] This accords with the scientific submission that human beings are six times more likely than the average mammal to kill one another, a propensity (to violence) which is an inherited trait.[48]

---

44 Ibid.

45 Eleanor Guetzloe, 'Origins of Violence and Aggression' (1997) available at https://education.wm.edu/centers/ttac/resources/articles/challengebehav/originviolenceaggress/index.php accessed 12 September 2020.

46 WHO, 'Definition and Typology of Violence' (2020) available at https://www.who.int/violenceprevention/approach/definition/en/#:~:text=%22the%20intentional%20use%20of%20physical,%2C%20maldevelopment%2C%20or%20deprivation.%22 accessed 13 September 2020.

47 C Sorrel, 'This History of Human Violence Explains How Society Shaped Killings' (2016) available at https://www.fastcompany.com/3064502/this-history-of-human-violence-explains-how-society-shaped-killing accessed 13 September 2020.

48 I Johnson, 'Humans Evolved to have an Instinct for Deadly Violence, (2016) available at https://www.independent.co.uk/news/science/human-evolution-violence-instinct-kill-murder-each-other-a7335491.html accessed 13 September 2020.

Perhaps, the most admitted case of earliest violence is that of Cain against Abel from Biblical history.[49] Violent wars between the city-states weakened the Sumerian rule in Mesopotamian civilization. Internal rebellions and frequent attacks of foreign forces caused bloodshed and unrest there. Violence in the Sumerian Civilization is reflected in the fact that "Sumerian city-states were constantly waging wars with one another."[50] Later on, Semitic King of the Akkad Sargon united the whole of Mesopotamia, but after his death, his empire "witnessed frequent attacks by barbarians coming from the desert regions."[51]

Violence was a distinct aspect of Greek Civilization as well. In 1200 BC, the whole of the city of Troy was demolished and razed to the ground. Homer, the famous Greek poet, has also described the destruction of this city in his epic poem, Iliad. He "pictures the war as caused by the abduction of a beautiful Greek woman" – Helen.[52] Violence was also a part and parcel of Roman society. The wars between Carthage and Rome are known as Punic Wars. The last Punic War was fought in 146 BC, and it caused the total destruction of Carthage. One can note the presence of violence in Roman society as games and sources of entertainment were full of violence. The Romans enjoyed violent shows like gladiatorial combat where men fought to their death. The spectacle was viewed by a large gathering including kings and queens.[53] It had the expressions of violence, bloodlust, and cruelty. Besides gladiatorial fights, criminals, rebels, and prisoners were punished in public gatherings there. They were thrown before a hungry lion. Julius Caesar's assassination in 44 BC by Brutus turned Rome into a battle field. Warlords and violent gangs became active and fought each other to seize power. Eventually, the situation took a turn for the worse as everything was subject to violence and disarray.[54]

Violence remained an integral part of the Middle Ages as well. Crusades were its big example. These were a series of wars fought between the Muslims

---

[49] Genesis, Chapter 4, verses 1-16.

[50] BV Rao, *World History* (New Delhi: Sterling Publishers Private Limited, 2004) 32.

[51] ibid

[52] Albert Hyma, *Ancient History* (New York: Barnes & Noble Inc., 1940) 62.

[53] Khalid Manzoor Butt and KanzaShareef, 'Violence in Historical Perspective' (n 2) above

[54] Ibid.

and Christians, lasted for almost two centuries and caused a lot of suffering. This series of crusades occurred mainly from 1095 to 1291.[55] The twentieth century has been regarded as the most violent century in the modern era. It experienced two world wars. Humanity suffered death and destruction on a large scale. World War I is the act of violence in the twentieth century, where three continents were involved. It was the first act of total war.[56] Since then, the world has also witnessed World War II, where violence was witnessed on a large scale, particularly in Hiroshima and Nagasaki. Here, the United States dropped atomic bombs that practically wiped out the two Japanese cities.[57]

Meaning of Violence

In ordinary usage, violence can be said to mean behaviour that is intended to hurt or kill somebody. It is the intentional use of physical force with the potential for causing death, disability, injury or harm.[58] Physical violence includes, but is not limited to, scratching, pushing, shoving and throwing, grabbing, biting, choking, shaking, slapping, punching, burning, use of weapons and use of restraints on one's body, size or strength against another person.[59] Violence and other forms of abuse are most commonly understood as a pattern of behaviour intended to establish and maintain control over family, household members, intimate partners, colleagues, individuals or groups.

The World Health Organization (WHO) considers violence as the intentional use of force or power, threatened or actual, against oneself or another person, which either results in or has a high likelihood of resulting in injury, death, psychological harm, mal-development or deprivation.[60] It is the over expression of physical force (with or without a weapon) against self or other, compelling action against one's will on pain of being hurt or killed or actually hurting or killing.[61] Violence is any act which causes or may cause any person

---

55 BV Rao (n 9) above

56 Norman Lowe, *Modern World History* (London: Macmillan Press Ltd., 1997), 101

57 Khalid Manzoor Butt and KanzaShareef, 'Violence in Historical Perspective' (n 2) above

58 United States Department of Health and Human Services, Centre for Disease Control and Prevention, accessed 13 April, 2018.

59 Ibid.

60 WHO, Definition and Typology of Violence (n 5) above.

61 G Gerbner and L Gross, *Violence in Television Drama: Trends and Symbolic Functions* (Comstock &Rubenstein, 1972), 400.

physical, psychological, emotional, sexual, verbal or economic harm whether these occur in private or public life, in peace time or in conflict situation.[62]

Violence as defined in the VAPP Act is any act or attempted act which causes or may cause any person physical, sexual, psychological, verbal, emotional or economic harm whether this occurs in private or public life, in peace time and in conflict situation.[63]

Domestic Violence

The concept of domestic violence is a relatively developing term with no unanimous agreement among writers on the meaning and scope of the concept. Many writers have used different expressions to describe violence between intimates. For some, it is a problem of women in marital relationships being assaulted, and the term 'wife abuse' or 'wife battering' is most appropriate. Others note that the real problem is the tacit societal acceptance of violence against women. After all, the act of battering occurs just as frequently among couples who are dating or living together but are not married.[64] Some writers are even assertive of the view that although injuries due to violence occur disproportionately against women and that men commit more serious violent acts, both genders engage in violence. For this reason, proponents of this perspective favour the gender-neutral terms domestic violence, domestic assault, intimate partner violence, or intimate partner assault because they are intrinsically less limiting. One of these proponents has defined domestic violence as violence between intimates living together or who have previously cohabited.[65]

Domestic violence in Nigeria is a problem affecting almost every part of the African continent; however, the situation in Nigeria is generally influenced by the prevailing cultural belief, especially among women. Violence against a wife is seen as a tool that a husband uses to chastise and improve her. The

---

[62] MT Ladan, 'Enforcement of Electoral Laws in Nigeria (2006), paper presented at a 2-day seminar on enforcement of electoral law and reduction of electoral violence in Nigeria, available at http://www.gamji.com/article6000/NEWS6681.htm accessed 17 April, 2018.

[63] Section 1

[64] ES Buzawa and CG Buzawa, *Domestic Violence: The Criminal Justice Response* (London: Sage Publications Ltd, 2002) 100-103

[65] Ibid.

Yoruba women refer to their husbands as '*olowoori mi*' meaning 'he owns me'. The act of marriage is culturally seen to give the husband full ownership of the wife, this is mainly symbolised in the payment of the bride price, thus making the man believe he is the overlord over the woman and all her rights are subject to his own convenience. Culture and cultural belief are therefore major factors for the recurring acts of domestic violence in Nigeria. The society cannot continue to fold hands to see domestic violence escalate like wild fire; the instrument of the law must be used to curb the rising trend of domestic violence in Nigeria, thus necessitating the enactment of the Violence Against Persons (Prohibition) Act of 2015 by the National Assembly.

Violence against Women and Girls

Women and girls in Nigeria face different levels of sexual and gender-based violence in both private and public life, often without protection from the law and even where law exists, it is hardly implemented to provide succour to victims. Compounding the problem of women and their rights is Nigeria's pluralist legal system, which includes Customary and Sharia Laws that often re-inforces sex stereotypes, including giving a man the right to batter the wife or make decisions on her behalf.

Violence against women and girls (VAWG), also known as gender-based violence and sexual and gender-based violence (SGBV) are violent acts the victims of which are primarily or exclusively women or girls. Such violence is often considered a form of hate crime, committed against women or girls specifically because they are female, and can take many forms. Violence against women means any act or attempted act of violence directed against women and girls which causes or may cause physical, sexual, psychological, verbal, emotional or economic harm whether this occurs in private or public life. The definition of violence against women has been broadened to include not just violent acts, such as physical assault, sexual assault, and threats of physical and sexual assault, but also non-violent acts, such as stalking and psychological, verbal and emotional abuse. Violence against women infringes on and impairs the enjoyment by women of their human rights and fundamental freedoms.

According to the 1993 UN Declaration on the Elimination of Violence against Women, Article 1 defines violence against women as "any act of gender-based violence – that is violence directed against a woman because she is a woman or that affects women disproportionately – that results in or is likely to result in physical, sexual or psychological harm or suffering to women, including threats of such acts, coercion or arbitrary deprivation of liberty, whether occurring in public or in private life." Under Article 2 of the Declaration, violence against women is understood to encompass, but not limited, to the following; a. Physical, sexual and psychological violence occurring in the family, including battering, sexual abuse of female children in the household, dowry-related violence, marital rape, female genital mutilation and other traditional harmful practices to women, non-spousal violence and violence related to exploitation; b. Physical, sexual and psychological violence occurring within the community, including rape, sexual abuse, sexual harassment and intimidation at work, in educational institutions and elsewhere, trafficking in women and forced prostitution; c. Physical, sexual and psychological violence perpetrated or condoned by the state, wherever it occurs.

The 1995 Beijing Platform for Action expanded the above definition by including the violations of the rights of women in situations of armed conflict, including systematic rape, sexual slavery and forced pregnancy, forced sterilisation, forced abortion, coerced or forced use of contraceptives; pre-natal sex selection and female infanticide.

The Role of Culture and Social Norms in Perpetuating Violence

Cultural and social norms are rules or expectations of behaviour within a specific cultural or social group. Often unspoken, these norms offer social standards of appropriate and inappropriate behaviour, governing what is (and is not) acceptable and co-ordinating our interactions with others.[66] Cultural and social norms persist within society because of individuals' preference to conform, given the expectation that others will also conform.[67] A variety of external and internal pressures maintain cultural and social norms.[68] Thus,

---

[66] SN Durlauf and LEBlume *New Palgrave Dictionary of Economics*, Second Edition (London, Macmillan, 2008); see also WHO (World Health Organization), *Changing cultural and social norms supportive of violent behaviour, Series of briefings on violence prevention: The Evidence* (Geneva, Switzerland: World Health Organization, 2009).

[67] D Lewis,*Convention: a Philosophical Study* (Cambridge MA: Harvard University Press, 1969).

[68] World Health Organization, *Changing cultural and social norms supportive of violent behaviour* (Series of *briefings on violence prevention: The Evidence* (Geneva, Switzerland: World Health Organization, 2009).

individuals are discouraged from violating norms by the threat of social disapproval or punishment and feelings of guilt and shame that result from the internalisation of norms. Cultural and social norms do not necessarily correspond with an individual's attitudes (positive or negative feelings towards an object or idea) and beliefs (perceptions that certain premises are true), although they may influence these attitudes and beliefs if norms become internalised. Cultural and social norms also vary widely; so, behaviour acceptable to one social group, gang or culture may not be tolerated in another.[69]

For instance, traditional beliefs that men have a right to control or discipline women through physical means makes women vulnerable to violence by intimate partners[70] and places girls at risk of sexual abuse.[71] Equally, cultural acceptance of violence, including sexual violence, as a private affair hinders outside intervention and prevents those affected from speaking out and gaining support.[72] In many societies, victims of sexual violence also feel stigmatised, which inhibits reporting.[73] Additionally, strong evidence of an association between alcohol consumption and violent behaviour means that cultural and social norms around alcohol use and its expected effects can also encourage and justify violent acts. In a number of countries, harmful alcohol use is estimated to be responsible for 26% of male and 16% of female disability-adjusted life-years lost as a result of homicide.[74] Societies that tolerate higher rates of acute alcohol intoxication report stronger relationships between

---

69 N Abrahams and R. Jewkes, Effects of South African men's having witnessed abuse of their mothers during childhood on their levels of violence in adulthood (2005) 95 *American Journal of Public Health*, 1811–1816.

70 A Mitra and P Singh,'Human capital attainment and gender empowerment: the Kerala paradox' (2007) 2007/88 Social Science Quarterly, 1227–1242; see also AL Ilika, 'Women's perception of partner violence in a rural Igbo community' (2005) 2005/9 African Journal of Reproductive Health, 77–88.

71 R Jewkes, L Penn-Kekana and H Rose-Junius,'"If they rape me, I can't blame them": reflections on gender in the social context of child rape in South Africa and Namibia' (2005) 61 Social Science and Medicine, 1809–1820

72 R Hussain and A Khan, 'Women's perceptions and experiences of sexual violence in marital relationships and its effect on reproductive health' (2008) 29 Health Care for Women International, 468–483.

73 MR Sable et al. Barriers to reporting sexual assault for women and men: perspectives of college students. Journal of American College Health, 2006, 55:157–162.

74 WHO global status report on alcohol 2004. Geneva, World Health Organization, 2004

alcohol use and violence than those where drinking occurs more moderately.[75] Furthermore, alcohol-related violence is considered more likely in cultures where many believe that alcohol plays a positive role by helping people to shed their inhibitions.[76] Here, alcohol can be used as a justification for violent behaviour, or consumed to fuel the courage needed to commit violent crimes. Interventions that tackle the cultural and social norms underlying risky drinking behaviour can help in preventing violence.[77]

Towards the Prohibiting of Violence against Persons in Nigeria

According to the 2018 Nigeria demographic and Health Survey (NDHS), approximately 31 per cent of women aged between 15 and 49 had experienced some form of physical violence since the age of 15, and 14 per cent had experienced physical violence in the 12 months preceding the survey.[78] The public opinion poll found that 54 per cent of Nigerians have suffered a form of domestic violence or know someone that has experienced domestic violence in their homes.[79] In a 2017 report, Nigeria's gender-based violence Sub-Sector working Group indicates that one of four ever-married women have reported having experienced at least one type of domestic violence such as physical, emotional or sexual violence by their husband or partner.[80]

As a result, human rights and women groups have, over the years, pushed for the passing of comprehensive legislation against gender-based violence/ violence against women. Their efforts in the past had either been rebuffed or stalled. Arguably, the coming together of these different groups eventually helped mobilise action to improve the legislative landscape for violence against

---

75 I Rossow, 'Alcohol and homicide: a cross-cultural comparison of the relationship in 14 European countries' (2001) 96 Addiction, 77–92.

76 D MacAndrew and RB, Edgerton, 'Drunken Comportment: a Social Explanation' (1969) Chicago, Aldine, Cited in EG Krug et al, *World Report on Violence and Health* (Geneva, World Health Organization, 2002)

77 See *Interpersonal Violence and Alcohol* (Geneva, World Health Organization and Centre for Public Health, Liverpool John Moores University, 2006) 17; Alcohol and Interpersonal Violence: Policy Briefing. (Copenhagen, World Health Organization (Regional Office for Europe) and Centre for Public Health, Liverpool John Moores University, 2005).

78 See NPC of Nigeria and ICF, October 2019, 429

79 NOIPolls Limited and Project Alert , July 2016, 4

80 gender-based violence Sub-Sector working Group (2017) 9.

women in Nigeria.[81] The result of that activism significantly contributed to the enactment of laws prohibiting violence against persons in Nigeria.

The Violence against Persons (Prohibition) Act, 2015 was signed into law on the 25th of May 2015 after over 10 years in the legislative process. It is an amalgamation of different bills which sought to abolish all obsolete laws relating to matters such as rape, assault etc. It aims to improve upon similar provisions on violence as contained in Nigeria's Criminal and Penal Code.[82] The Act is the first criminal legislation in Nigeria to expand the concept of rape beyond penetration of the vagina and anus by the penis and to include penetration of the mouth by the penis. The VAPP Act is also the first instrument to prohibit and punish female genital mutilation, forced eviction by a person of his/her spouse and children, verbal, emotional and psychological abuses, harmful widowhood practices, political violence, amongst others.

The Violence Against Persons (Prohibition) Act, 2015 is a national law and its provisions are applicable throughout the country.[83] This is a significant development because of the previously detached nature of law against violence, particularly gender-based violence. The Act defines violence as any act or attempted act, which causes or may cause any person physical, sexual, psychological, verbal, emotional or economic harm whether this occurs in private or public life, in peace time and in conflict situations.[84] The definition appears all encompassing as it captures every form of imaginable nature of violence like violence against men, women, children, political violence et cetera. The VAPP Act is an Act enacted to eliminate violence in private and public life, prohibit all forms of violence against persons and to provide maximum protection and effective remedies for victims and punishment of offenders. The Act provides for 26 Offences, and is divided

---

[81] Cheluchi Onyemelukwe, 'Legislating on Violence against Women: A Critical Analysis of Nigeria's Recent Violence against Persons (Prohibition) Act, 2015' (2016) 5 DePaul J. Women, Gender & L., 3.

[82] C Onyemelukwe and I Okekeogbu, 'The Violence against Persons (Prohibition) Act: A CHELD Brief' (Centre for Health Ethics Law and Development (CHELD), 2015) available at www.cheld.org accessed 15 May, 2016

[83] Taiye Joshua Omidiyin, 'Violence Against Persons (Prohibition) Act 2015: A Positive Step To The Eradication Of Domestic Violence In Nigeria' (2018) 9/1 NAUJILJ, 39 at 46

[84] Violence against Persons (Prohibition) Act, 2015 s.1

into six parts. Section 46 of the Act incorporates the rights guaranteed under the Constitution.

On the other hand, the Enugu State Violence Against Persons Prohibition Law, 2019 was a private member bill (House Bill No. 15, 2017) meant to eliminate all forms of violence against persons for both public and private lives. The bill was enacted into law on 8th May 2019 with the Governor's assent. The law is made up of five parts and 45 sections.

Comparing the Violence against Persons (Prohibition) Act, 2015 and the Enugu State Violence against Persons Prohibition Law, 2019

Many provisions of the 2019 Enugu State Law are reproductions of the provisions of the 2015 Federal Act. Both legislation cover similar offences including rape, physical violence/injury, psychological, economic and political violence, coercion, harmful traditional practices, amongst others. They also deal with issues of jurisdiction of courts, service providers and regulatory authorities.

Nevertheless, there are areas where the laws diverge. It is to these differences that this paper will now turn to.

Definition of Rape

According to section 1 (1) (a) of the 2015 Act, rape is committed where a person intentionally penetrates the vagina, anus or mouth of another person **with any other part of his or her body or anything else** and the other person does not consent to the penetration or such consent is obtained by means of threat or intimidation of any kind or by fear of harm. For the 2019 Enugu Law, section 3 (1) (a) provides that a person commits rape where **he** intentionally penetrates the vagina, anus or mouth of another person **no matter how slight with his sex organ** or any other part of his body or anything else.

The use of "he or she" in the 2015 Act clearly means that both genders may be perpetrators of violence for the purpose of the Act. However, the use of "he" in the Enugu State law has the capacity to bring confusion. The 2015 Act is therefore better couched in this regard. Again, the inclusion of the phrase "no matter how slight" appears to be an upgrade on the definition in the 2015 Act, which does not contain the phrase.

Protective Order

In section 28 of the 2015 Act, an application for a protective order may be made before a high court following a complaint of violence by the complainant and such order, if granted, shall be effective throughout the Federal Republic of Nigeria and no time limit or prescription shall apply in relation to a person seeking to apply for such order. Under section 24 of the Enugu state 2019 Law, an application for protective order may be made before any competent court following a complaint of violence by the complainant. A protection order granted by **any High Court of Magistrate Court** shall be effective throughout Enugu State and no time limit or prescription shall apply for such protective order.

The Enugu State 2019 Law includes Magistrate Courts as those with capacity to grant protective orders. This is missing in the 2015 Act. Again, naturally, while the 2015 act applies nationally, the 2019 Law applies only within Enugu State.

Sex Offenders' Register

Section 1 (4) of the 2015 Federal legislation provides that a register for convicted offenders shall be maintained and accessible to the public. There is no equivalent provision in the 2019 Enugu State Law.

The thinking is that this register is necessary, in order to easily identify those who have been convicted of offences of this nature. It is therefore necessary to have a law that creates this register, even at the State level. In this context, the omission of this provision from the 2019 Enugu state Law is unfortunate.

Power to Conduct Finger Prints/DNA Tests

Under section 32 (3) (c) of the 2015 Act, Police officer shall have the power to collect and store finger prints including DNA of accused and convicted offenders. However, there is no equivalent provision in the Enugu State Law of 2019. There is no explanation in the law as to why this paragraph is omitted from the 2019 Law.

Seizure of Arms and Dangerous Weapons

The provisions of section 30 of the 2019 Enugu State Law provides that the court shall order a member of the Nigerian Police Force to seize any arm or dangerous weapon in the possession or under the control of a respondent, if the court is satisfied on the evidence placed before it, including any affidavits supporting an application, that the respondent has threatened or expressed intention to kill or injure himself or herself or any person in a domestic relationship, whether or not by means of such arm or dangerous weapon.

This is a novel provision in the State law which has no equivalent in the Federal Act of 2015. Without doubt, this provision is a good one, as it is a proactive action that has the capacity to prevent the execution of violence on persons. Nevertheless, it may also be argued that the Police, by virtue of the duties ascribed to them by law (for instance the Police Act), already have such powers to carry out this function and asking the court to carry out this function is merely superfluous.

Protection Officers

Under section 41 of the 2015 Federal Act, Protection officers are to deal with Police and accredited service providers in Area Councils. On the other hand, in section 37 of the 2019 Enugu State Law, Protection officers in Local Government Councils deal with accredited service providers in local governments. Again, in section 42 of the 2015 Act, the Co-ordinator is mandated to submit Annual Reports to the Federal Government. In section 38 of the 2019 Enugu State Law, the Co-ordinator is enjoined to submit Report to the State Government.

Regulatory Agencies

By the provisions of section 44 of the 2015 Federal legislation, The National Agency for the Prohibition of Trafficking in Persons and other Related Matters (NAPTIP) is mandated to administer the provisions of the Act. Under section 40 of the 2019 Enugu State Law, The Agency on Violence against Persons (Agency) is established as a body corporate with perpetual seal, capable of suing and being sued in its own name and with the capacity to acquire, hold and dispose of any movable property for the purpose of carrying out its function. Section 41 of the same law stipulates the functions of the Agency, which shall include monitoring and supervising the implementation of the provisions of the law; creating directories of service; recruiting staff for the Agency; providing and managing victims crises centres; registering accredited service providers; and performing other functions as may be specified by any law or enactment, amongst others.

Trust Fund for the Agency

Section 45 of the same 2019 Law establishes a Trust Fund for the Agency. The trust Fund is for the purpose of providing aid for victims of violence through rehabilitation of victims individually or as a group; reintegrating the victim into the society; provision of shelter and legal aid, among other things. There is no equivalent provision in the Federal 2015 legislation creating a Trust Fund for the NAPTIP. In this context, the Enugu State law is an improvement on the 2015 Act as the Trust Fund (if effectively implemented) will enable the regulatory Agency to carry out its responsibilities in a more efficient manner. Apart from these major differences, there also minor variations between the two legislation. This is especially true in the area of degree of punishment to which convicted offenders are subjected to. These include:

Conviction for the Offence of Rape

Under section 1 (2) of the 2015 Act, where the offender is below the age of 14, the person shall be remanded in a remand home or appropriate place and for a number of years as the judge deems fit. For the Enugu State Law, section 4 stipulates that the Judge can only do so where the offender is below the age of 18 years.

In this context, the threshold for sending an offender to a remand home is higher in the Enugu State Law. Considering the prevalence of violence in Nigeria today (especially against women and girls) and the fact that it seems children mature faster now than before, the provision of the 2015 Act is preferred.

Attempt to Commit Violence (inflicting physical injury)

Under section 2 (2) of the 2015 Act, any person who attempts to commit violence (inflicting physical injury on a person) is liable to three years imprisonment or fine of N200,000 However, section 5 (2) of the Enugu State law provides that any person who attempts to commit offence provided for in section 1 shall be liable on conviction to a term not exceeding five years or fine of N50,000 or to both.

Offensive Conduct

Section 5 (1) of the 2015 Act states that any person who compels another, by force or threat, to engage in any conduct or act, sexual or otherwise to the detriment of the victim's physical/psychological well-being commits an offence liable on conviction to a term not exceeding two years imprisonment and or fine not exceeding N500,000 or both. On the other hand, section 8 of the 2019 Enugu Law provides for a term of imprisonment not exceeding three years or fine not exceeding N100,000 or both.

Harmful Widowhood Practices

Section 15 of the 2015 Act insists that any person who subjects a widow to harmful traditional practices commits an offence and is liable on conviction to a term of imprisonment not exceeding two years or to a fine not exceeding N500,000 or both. Where there is an attempt to commit the offence in section 15, the punishment is imprisonment not exceeding one year or fine of N200,000 or both. For the Enugu State law, section 14 provides for imprisonment not exceeding two years or fine not exceeding N200,000 or both. Where there is an attempt, imprisonment should not exceed one year or fine not exceeding N100,000 or both.

From the foregoing on the capacity of offenders and the degree of punishment available, it is obvious that the 2015 federal legislation contains a more stringent punishment for convicted offenders. Bearing in mind that violence should be deterred by all means, it is the thinking of this presenter that the legislation with a heavier punishment scheme is the better option. In this context, the Enugu State Law, which is even later in time, ought to have contained a punishment regime that is heavier, when compared with the federal Act. Unfortunately, this is not so and as a result, the overriding supposition is that the state law should be amended to increase the punishment regime contained in it.

Conclusion

Before 2015, most of the extant laws in Nigeria on prohibiting violence against persons were outdated and insufficiently comprehensive, neither specifically directed to this grave problem nor adequately enforced. The development of law in the fight against domestic violence in Nigeria, therefore, became a matter that needed to be urgently addressed, thus leading to the enactment of the Violence against Persons (Prohibition) Act, 2015. The passing into law of this legislation is a remarkable step in the right direction. Many States of the Federation have followed suit and enacted their own Laws, prohibiting violence against persons. Enugu State, in 2019, enacted its own Law which prohibits violence against persons. While there are many similarities between the Act of 2015 and the Enugu State Law of 2019 (that is, many of the provision of the Enugu State law is a reproduction of the provisions of the 2015 Act), it is also true that there are areas of divergence between the two laws. This paper has pointed out these similarities and identified the areas of divergence. Essentially, a holistic evaluation of the laws reveals that they are meant to operate alongside some international instruments signed and ratified by the country to curb violence against persons in Nigeria.

Nevertheless, these laws, by themselves will have limited impacts, unless there is an intensive advocacy by all stakeholders to ensure their effective implementation. This author believes that these laws have the potential to provide effective protections for persons (especially women and girls) against gender-based violence. However, specific actions will need to be taken to move the laws from words on paper to active implementation and protection of persons (especially women) from gender-based violence in Nigeria. Enforcement of the legislation must be taken seriously. Nigeria has a poor record on enforcement of extant laws. Law enforcement officials (especially the Police) must be consistently reminded of their obligations. Issues of violence must no longer be termed private matters. It is only when these steps are taken that the purpose for which these laws were enacted would be realised.

POLICE PROTECTION OF WOMEN IN NIGERIA

By
Amucheazi Chibike Oraeto

Faculty of Law, University of Nigeria, Enugu Campus

ABSTRACT

Women in Nigeria face numerous challenges under various extant laws and customs. However most of the challenges are basically discriminatory practices which invariably stem from the cultural background of the country. It is basically the culture of the country, which features various customary and religious sects, that exalts such discriminatory practices. This leaves the male folk as the dominant sex for which it is the common supposition today that Nigeria is a patriarchal state. Nevertheless, this paper focuses on an aspect of our legal jurisprudence regarding the protection of women in our society. The paper takes on this theme from the perspective of sexual assault, which has become a horror for women in Nigeria. It highlights the Violence against Persons (Prohibition) Act and while it applauds the domestication of the law in Enugu State, it nevertheless pontificates on the apparent short comings of the Law. These shortcomings are essentially centred on the protection of women in the area of sexual assaults. The paper contends that notwithstanding the administration of the VAPP Law and the consequent reforms it may bring; the subsistence of certain legal materials such as police methods of investigation and general attitude still impacts negatively on prosecution of sexual assault cases. The methodology adopted in the study is of a qualitative nature and consists of library based texts analysis.

INTRODUCTION

The passing into law of the Violence against Persons (Prohibition) Law in Enugu State as elsewhere[85] is a good development. This followed the enactment of the Violence against Persons (Prohibition) (VAPP) Act, 2015, by the National Assembly. The law seeks to eliminate all forms of violence against persons in both public and private lives. The law is indeed a good development, especially in the Covid-19 era. However, following the corona virus attack, the nation has been under a lockdown. This has caused a decline in the nation's economic status and presents psychological disturbances for citizens of the country. Consequently, it does seem that the merits of the VAPP legislation are challenged by an increase of crime in the nation.[86] The violence which the Act seeks to eliminate is now heightened by virtue of the corona virus pandemic in the country. Most disturbing, however, is the crime of rape which a quick search on *Google* shows that it has become rampant in Nigeria within the last few months, reaching a peak in the last week of May 2020 and the first week of June.[87] The story is the same globally as Nigeria followed Pakistan and Nepal as top spots for rape cases from *Google* trends. Nigeria is the only African nation in the top ranking search for rape issues within the last few months.[88] A report has it that in the last few weeks, rape cases in Nigeria had involved minors. For instance, a 12-year-old girl was raped by four masked men in her home in Ajah, Lagos. The incident occurred few days after Uwaila Vera Omozuwa, a student of the University of Benin was raped and killed.[89] There is now the trending discussion of male rape, but this is not the focus of this paper.

Apart from the Covid-19 pandemic, a major reason for the increase in certain crimes, such as violations of women's rights in Nigeria, is the issue of the

---

[85] However only few states have signed the Act into law and as at June 2020, 23 States hold back signing on the VAPP Act. See https://www.google.com/amp/s/www.dataphyte.com/gender/its-not-freedom-for-women-in-nigeria-as-states-hold-back-signing-on-the-violence-against-persons-prohibition-act/%3famp_markup=1 accessed 10/9/2020.

[86] See BBC News "Crime during coronavirus" available at https://www.google.com/amp/s/www.bbc.com/pidgin/tori-52196311.amp accessed 10/9/2020.

[87] See Dataphyte report at https://www.google.com/amp/s/www.dataphyte.com/gender/its-not-freedom-for-women-in-nigeria-as-states-hold-back-signing-on-the-violence-against-persons-prohibition-act/%3famp_markup=1 accessed 10/9/2020.

[88] Ibid

[89] Op cit note 4.

existing cultures in Nigeria that support the subjugation of women. It may be true that the reason why there is subjugation of women in Nigeria is due to lack of comprehensive understanding of the order of the law. It does seem that our customary practices, which in most cases are gender unfriendly, are placed first even before the extant laws. It is for this that a part of this paper briefly addresses the basis for protection of women in our society. The basis is founded upon the order of nature and our laws are crested upon that order.

The fundamental questions are: *what law guarantees and speaks for the rights of women and girls in Nigeria? What institutions guarantee the protection of women and girls? Why is there an increase in rape cases in Nigeria? What is the sure way to circumvent crime in any society and ultimately what is the basis for protection of women and girls in our society?*

JURISPRUDENTIAL ANALYSIS OF THE BASIS FOR PROTECTION OF WOMEN

Law itself is an expression of culture and both the law and culture are dynamic and evolving.[90] Culture permeates all human activities and institutions, including legal systems in all societies across the world, but culture is created, contested and recreated within the social and political arenas. Perhaps a consistent review of our constitutional jurisprudence is necessary in order to recreate certain customs that are not in consonance with globally acceptable laws and that are apparently gender-biased. These global laws are essentially entrenched in the natural law order which is common to all humans. Natural law is a theory in ethics and philosophy that stipulates that human beings possess intrinsic values that govern our reasoning and behaviour. Natural law maintains that the principles or rules of right and wrong are inherent in people and are not created by society or court judges. Indeed no declaration of human right will ever be exhaustive and final. It will ever go hand-in-hand with the state of moral consciousness. A natural law moral theory gives an account of the way in which first principles of practical reason take on a moral force by being considered through a united "*directiveness*". That integral "*directiveness*" is given specific articulation in principles such as the injunction to love one's neighbor as oneself; or the golden rule of doing to others what you would want to be done to you. It also charges on the

[90] Geertz 1983.

categorical imperatives to report and treat as intrinsically valuable, humanity in oneself and others, so that each person, whether male or female, is treated with respect, dignity and equality.[91]

However to grant the right of respect and dignity which derives from the natural law of reason, it is pertinent to identify with the institutions of governmental authority. The political-theoretical part of natural law theory explains and elaborates the grounds for proper forms of governmental authority. It shows the need for instituting and accepting practical authority as an almost invariably necessary means of preventing forms of neglect and abuse which involve injustice. The jurisprudential political theory applied in societies explains the normal desirability that governmental authority in political communities be exercised within the framework of a rule of law predicated on natural reason and not the rule of men.[92]

Perhaps, the application of the rule of men in a patriarchal society such as ours has corrupted our inherent understanding of natural law and leaves us to resort to customary rules created by men. Yet political authority remains a remedy for injustice and impoverishment. The extant laws must be enforced by the authorities (such as the police) and it is important for the institutions to identify portions of our positive law which consists of natural legal principles (*such as the fundamental human rights provisions as contained in the 1999 Constitution of Nigeria*). These natural legal principles expose us to the knowledge of moral standards that are conceptual necessities. One of the necessities is the protection of women against sexual assaults. The basis, therefore, for the protection of women is that there is a natural law injunction against discrimination on grounds of sex as well as a rule of equality amongst humans.

It is clear that the institutions of authority in a state are in service of substantive purposes such as upholding the rule of equality; protection of humans against discrimination as well as sexual assault or other forms of exploitation. Yet, the offence of rape is still on the increase and these government institutions may not

---

91 Stanford Encycloeadia of Philosophy, Natural Law Theories, *First published Mon Feb 5, 2007; substantive revision Wed Jun 3, 2020*

92 Stanford Encycloeadia of Philosophy, Natural Law Theories, *First published Mon Feb 5, 2007; substantive revision Wed Jun 3, 2020*

have very well protected the victims who are mostly women. Below is a chart that provides information on the rate of the crime of rape in Nigeria in 2020.

RAPE CASES IN 2020

Oyo, Akwa Ibom, and Ekiti States top recent brutal rape cases in recent weeks. According to *Daily Trust*, Nigeria has recorded more than 60 reported cases of rape between January and June. Among these figures, 23 are minors, 25 are teens, and six adults. Victims are yet to get justice for their acts. Dataphyte compiled some of the recently reported cases of rape in Nigeria:

No	States	Victims	Cases
1	Oyo	Barakat Bello	Raped and killed at home, Akinyele LG, Ibadan
2	Oyo	Grace Oshiagwu	Rape and Killed at home, Akinyele LG Ibadan
3	Edo	Vera Uwaila Omozuwa;	Raped and killed inside a Redeemed Christian Church of God in Benin city.
4	Jigawa	A 12-year-old girl (Name withheld)	12 men had sexual intercourse with her at different times, including a 67-year old man.
5	Ekiti	17-year-old girl	Gang-raped by local boys while hawking sachet water in Ado Ekiti.
6	Ekiti	3-year-old girl	Defiled by a 15-year-old boy in Osi Ekiti.
7	Lagos	12-year old	Four masked men raped the victim in Ajah Lagos
8	Cross River	4-year-old niece	Captain Bassey Ekanem (retd) for defiling his four-year-old niece in Calabar.

9	Akwa Ibom	13-year-old girl	Godwin Jeremiah, her father, sexually assaulted and raped her repeatedly in their home in Eket.
10	Akwa Ibom	15-year-old step-daughter	55-year-old man, Udo Ekong Esau forcefully slept with his step-daughter in Uyo.
11	Kaduna	13-year-old girl	Four men gang-raped, drugged her, gang-raped, and later dumped her under a parked vehicle near her home.
12	Benue	11-year-old housemaid	Medical doctor raped 11-year-old housemaid.

Table Adapted From Dataphyte Report On Google[93]

HOW DO WE ELIMINATE THIS VIOLENCE AND DEFILEMENT OF THE WOMAN?

The first approach, perhaps, is to identify the law that guarantees and speaks for the rights of women and girls in Nigeria. Under Nigerian law, women have been accorded some legal protections. Basically, these rights are provided for under the Nigerian Constitution and other international treaties and conventions to which Nigeria is a party. There is also the general constitutional rights of men and also inclusive are the rights of women to freedom from discrimination. This right is provided for under section 42(1) of the 1999 Constitution. In specific terms section 42 (1) (a) prohibits the subjection of an individual to discrimination on account of his place of origin, sex, religion, etc. Section 42 (1) (b) prohibits the privileges or disadvantages to any citizen based on the same ground as mentioned above. There is also the Fundamental Objectives and Directive Principles of State Policy as provided

---

93 https://www.google.com/amp/s/www.dataphyte.com/gender/its-not-freedom-for-women-in-nigeria-as-states-hold-back-signing-on-the-violence-against-persons-prohibition-act/%3famp_markup=1 accessed 9/10/20.

under the same constitution. These objectives serve as guides to the Nigerian Government and the citizens, and prohibit any form of discrimination on grounds of place of origin, sex, religion, status, ethnic or linguistic association or ties.[94]

With regards to rape, section 283 of the Penal Code and section 282 of the Criminal Code specifically provides for protection for the chastity of women. Another legislation which provides for the rights of women in Nigeria is the Labor Act, amongst others. Today, the focus is on the VAPP Act and it is hoped that much good will come from its administration. Sadly, only a few states have passed the Act into law.

These laws mentioned above provide for legal rights of women. But what really is a legal right? Although the term denotes different meaning to different people, it generally means any right which has the legal protection of law and if breached or violated, incurs liability. Muftau defines a legal right as one which has been clothed with full protection of law, and if breached or trampled upon, the person, affected by the breach can seek redress in a law court.[95] Muftau's definition of a legal right is instructive because it immediately spurs the question as to whom the duty to implement the laws and protect the citizen falls upon. This essentially brings us to the next question in this paper; what institutions guarantee the protection of women and girls?

First, it is important to mention that the implementation of the laws that seek to protect women is challenged by religious commandments and existing cultures in Nigeria that are often at variance with extant provisions of the various laws. There is also the challenge of the inadequacy of provisions in the laws. The VAPP Act, for instance, fails to address the area of standards of investigations in sexual assault cases that will maintain the integrity of a woman/victim.

However, what seems obvious is that the legislature and civil society organisations continue to play their part in enhancing the scope and breadth of laws that protect women in our society. It remains for the executive arm

---

94 See section 15(2) of the 1999 Constitution of FRN.

95 See Dr Rufai Muftau "An Appraisal of the Legal Rights of Women in Nigeria" Journal of Law, Policy and Globalization, Vol 52, 2016.

of government to play its role of implementation of the laws. The primary institution charged with the protection of women and girls in Nigeria is the Nigerian Police Force. The protection of women and girls can be achieved by a proper implementation of the laws through viable prosecution of offenders. Sexual assault and violation of women can be circumvented through prosecution which obviously deters offenders. Prosecution and conviction of offenders remains one of the most practicable means of crime prevention and control.[96] This is one sure way to circumvent crime in any society. Nevertheless, the Police can only prosecute when cases or incidents of abuse and violations are reported on time. There are indications that sexual assault offences are not promptly reported in Nigeria.[97] This situation has impacted negatively on prosecution of cases. The development is already affecting the VAPP Act as its aim is apparently defeated if victims cannot make prompt reports. This is the area that concerns the police and below extrapolates on the point of delay in connection with the police force.

WHY THE DELAY IN REPORTING SEXUAL OFFENCES?

It has been shown that citizens are to report crimes to the police, which equally are saddled with the responsibility to investigate and prosecute offenders. However, there has been an explosion of accusations from individuals who have experienced different forms of sexual harassment and rape and on many occasions, the disclosures concerned incidents that took place years ago.[98]

These delays in reporting often raise doubts among some regarding the veracity of the claims which consequently occasion the belief that some reports have political undertones. The effect of delay in report of rape can be overwhelming to a criminal adjudicatory system since factually during investigation of a rape allegation such delay makes it difficult to secure forensic evidence. Delay in

---

96 Daniel S. Nag in 'Deterrence in the Twenty-First Century' National Institute of Justice, June 5, 2016.

97 By the Eighth United Nations Survey on Crime Trends and the Operations of Criminal Justice Systems, there are still delays in report. UNODC.org.

98 In Nigeria, Mrs Bukola Dakolo reported that she was raped severally 20 years ago by the prominent Pastor Biodun Fatayinbo of the COZA Church. BBC News- https://www.google.com/amp/s/ww.bbafrica-47234844 Accessed 13/9/2020.

report may lead to incoherent and distorted statements and information that may not be helpful to the police.[99] The pertinent questions put across to a victim relates to who the offender is and where the offence took place as well as when it occurred. To this end, it is both valid and realistic to submit that delay in reporting cases of sexual assault adversely affects the prosecution of such offence and of course the entire adjudicatory process beginning from the investigation stage.

WHAT THEN IS THE REASON FOR DELAY AS IT CONCERNS THE POLICE?

The above discussion of late reports represents the realities on delay in report of rape incidences by victims. For emphasis, the question may be asked, "why do victims of rape delay before reporting to the police and law enforcement agencies?" Some of the reasons are as follows: victims fear attacks and retaliation especially in the absence of a viable security system that protects crime reporters. Some victims of rape assume that the incident is private and as such tend to avoid the consequential stigmatisation that may come with going public at the instance of the Police. As much as possible, victims expect that a report will remain confidential, yet the assumption is that the police and/or press may reveal the incident. Again, the adjudicatory process puts a victim on a strict proof of non-consent and the system consciously expects that there must be proof and visual evidence of physical injuries to sustain an allegation of rape. This may be apparently discomforting to the female victim. more so, proceedings are not private and are conducted in open court. There is also the possibility that the victim may be faulted by the police as being partly responsible for the mistreatment received, sometimes due to dressing or social conduct.

Generally, victims of rape are more likely to promptly report rape incidents if assured that the benefits of disclosure will outweigh its costs in terms of social stigmatisation; cost and time of resolving cases in court as well as privacy and confidentiality of the prosecution. It is instructive to note that the Nigerian Police and Judiciary are key factors that must offer such assurances to victims.

[99] Bavich M.T., Mackenzie K.L, Depue B.E, Whitner A.J., Miller G.A., Heller W., 'Cognitive Control Mechanisms, Emotion and Memory: A Neural Perspective with Implications for Psychopathology' (2009) 33 (5) Neuroscience and Bio-behavioral Reviews 613-630).

To further buttress the points above, the outcome of a research conducted by the *National Violence against Women Survey (NVAWS)*[100] reveals certain disclosures made by victims of rape as to the reason why they delay in reporting: 22 per cent cited fear of the perpetrator as a reason for not reporting; 18 per cent cited that they were too ashamed or embarrassed; 18 per cent felt that the incidence was a minor and not a major crime or a police matter; 13 per cent believed that the law enforcement agency could not do anything; and 12 per cent believed that the police officers would not believe but blame them. These responses are instructive for community professionals because they provide a glimpse into the perceptions of the public about how they will be treated if they report a rape incident, particularly, whether the report will be taken seriously and investigated thoroughly.

Many victims of rape therefore prefer not to disclose their experiences due to overwhelming fear, pain, self-doubt and shame. As aforementioned, in Nigeria, victims of rape find themselves embedded in a culture that commonly discounts their experiences and excuses the behaviour of their assailants. They may continue to fear for their own safety and face real dangers if they report to the authorities due to the poor security system that offers no protection to the crime reporter. This, therefore, is a wake-up call for the Police to again re-affirm their resolve to protect the woman especially in the area of sexual assaults. It has been stated that the law and prosecution remains a sure way to circumvent assault of the woman. It is essential for the legislature and judiciary to continue to play their role but most importantly the police will have to ensure that their role is played with the highest level of professionalism. After all the police remains vital to the criminal adjudicatory process.

WHAT THE POLICE MUST DO? (Observations and Recommendations)

It is, perhaps, important to reiterate that rape is still on the increase in Nigeria. Punishing crimes still offers a better deterrence but police methods of investigation and attitude towards the woman victim may be obstacles that merely prevent scores of sexual assault cases from being reported and prosecuted. The police remain essentially a part of a society with a culture

---

[100] National Victim Centre (1992) Rape in America: A Report to the Nation. Arlington, V.A: National Victim Centre and Crime Victims Research and Treatment Centre. http://www.evawintl.org//library/DocumentlibraryHander.ashx?id=538. Accessed 13/9/2020.

of subjugating women, but it must not permit itself to be influenced by that culture. It is important to begin to tackle the social factors that apparently cause delay in reporting. As issues concerning rape are matters that have to do with the human conscience, we must consider the consequences of delay in report of the offence. Apparently, as recent statistics show that women still delay in reporting the crime, it means that we have all failed to protect the woman.

As earlier mentioned, the focus of a State should be on addressing the social and psychological factors that cause delay in reports of rape. It is recommended that as a result of the proliferation of rape occurrences in Nigeria, as elsewhere, a special court be established to prosecute perpetrators of rape in order to accelerate proceedings and circumvent the worrisome delay that is discomforting to litigants. Proceedings in the special court can also be *conducted in camera* to ensure confidentiality. This will help eliminate stigmatisation as well as build confidence in rape survivors to come forward to report and diligently pursue their claims. As the police play a fundamental role in prosecution of cases, the above may be achieved if the authorities of the police consistently recommend for a special court.

More so, it is observed that the activities of the Nigerian Police Force are not technically monitored. It is recommended that the Nigerian Police officers be trained consistently and monitored closely in order to enhance professionalism. It is suggested that an official body camera device be worn by police officers. In response to the lack of trust and confidence in the police, American communities and legislators called for all officers to use body-worn cameras (BWCs) so that all interactions with civilians are recorded.[101] It is also necessary to conduct a routine appraisal to ensure that reporting the crime of rape to the police is evidentially taken serious and treated as required by globally accepted standards.[102]

---

101 See Jennifer L. Doleac, 'Do body Worn Cameras improve police behavior? Brookings, Wednesday (25 October 2017) https://www.brookings.edu/blog/up-front/2017/10/25/do-body-worn-cameras-improve-police-behaviour/amp/ accessed 14/9/2020.

102 Current research suggests that body-worn cameras may offer benefits for law enforcement and as it is viewed as one way to improve law enforcement practice more generally. See Brett Chapman, '*Body-Worn Cameras: What the Evidence Tells Us*', National Institute of Justice (NIJ), 14 November 2018.

In addition, it may be necessary to establish a gender desk in police stations manned by trained female police officers to enhance sensitivity and necessary consideration to report of rape incidents. Perhaps, the recent move by the presidency to overhaul the management and activities of the Special Anti-Robbery Squad division of the Nigerian Police is a step in the right direction. This may be extended to the Criminal Investigation Department (CID) and other units of the Nigerian police Force.[103]

Further, there should be a proper training of officers through viable and sustainable exchange programmes and cross border interconnection with countries with an advanced policing network and system such as the GIZ programme in Rwanda on behalf of the German Federal Foreign Office designed to strengthen the capacities of police structures in Africa.[104] This will enhance victim-reporter protection and dispel the fear of reprisal attacks usually entertained by rape survivors which will consequently promote early report of rape incidents.

Again, the Nigerian Police must engage citizens in social orientation programmes designed to repel the culture of shaming victims of rape. This can be achieved by a synergy with the Ministry responsible for women and children affairs as well as the National Orientation Agency.[105]

Finally, a review of our constitutional jurisprudence is necessary in order to recreate certain customs that are not in consonance with globally acceptable laws. These global laws are essentially entrenched in the natural law order which is common to all humans. We thus applaud the creation of the VAPP Act and hope that the Police as a government institution will consider the observations and recommendations herein and do the needful to protect our women.

---

[103] 'Osibanjo orders IGP to overhaul SARS' *Punch newspapers* (14 August 2018) <https://punchng.com> accessed 14/9/2020.

[104] The GIZ, '*Strengthening the capacity of Police structures in Africa*' Programme, commissioned by the German Foreign Affairs Office in Rwanda and executed by the Rwanda Ministry of Internal Security <https://www.giz.de/en/worldwide/20779.html> accessed 31 December 2019.

[105] The National Orientation Agency of Nigeria is the body tasked with communicating government policy, staying abreast of public opinion, and promoting patriotism, national unity, and development of the Nigerian Society.

POLICE POWER UNDER THE ENUGU STATE VAPP LAW (2019): EVIDENCE PRESERVATION, FACT FINDING AND INTERROGATION IN CASES OF VAWG.

By
Ndubuisi Nwafor

Abstract

This paper looks at the powers of the Police as contained in the Violence against persons (Prohibition) Law of Enugu State 2019. It argues that as a result of the enormous powers conferred on the Police by the Law, these law enforcement enforcers are enjoined to properly use their powers to effectively administer the VAPP Law in Enugu State. They are also encouraged to desist from excessive and unreasonable use of force in the conduct of their assignments.

Background

The Nigeria Police is a product of constitutional creation. There are some extant laws in Nigeria which, apart from the Constitution, also provide for the regulation and enforcement of powers of the Nigeria Police Force. They include: the 1999 Federal Republic of Nigeria Constitution; the Nigeria Police Act, CAP P19, LFN 2004; Administration Of Criminal Justice Act, 2015 (now the Administration Of Criminal Justice Law of various states which domesticated it); the Violence Against persons (prohibition) Act (VAPP) (now also The Violence Against Persons (Prohibition) Law by various states which domesticated it);[106] Evidence Act[107], 2011; etc. Presently, Nigeria operates a federal system of government, the implication of this is that structurally, Nigeria is made up of the central federal government and other federating units called the state government. Section 2(2) of the 1999 Constitution (Amended) of the Federal Republic of Nigeria[108] provides that 'Nigeria shall be a Federation consisting of States and Federal Capital Territory'. The legal implication of the above is that there are certain items which are exclusively under the control and management of the federal government. One of the most important of such items is policing. Section 214 (1) of the 1999 Constitution provides that:

> There shall be a Police Force for Nigeria, which shall be known as the Nigerian Police Force, and subject to the provisions of this section no other police force shall be established for the federation or any part thereof.

It is right to argue that Nigeria does not permit anything but a federal police force system. This argument can be buttressed by the provision of section 214(2) a of the 1999 Constitution which provides that:

> The Nigeria Police Force shall be organized and administered in accordance with the provisions as may be prescribed by an Act of the National Assembly.

The Nigeria National Assembly, which is the federal law making organ of the Nigeria government, is bestowed with the duties and obligations to exclusively make laws pertaining to the administration of the Nigeria Police Force. This fact is supported under item 45 of the Second Schedule, Part 1, of 1999

---

[106] https://lawpavilion.com/blog/the-violence-against-persons-prohibition-act-2015/

[107] https://www.refworld.org/pdfid/54f86b844.pdf

[108] The 1999 Constitution of the Federal Republic of Nigeria is the supreme law that governs Nigeria. Section 1 of the Constitution provides that "This Constitution is supreme and its provisions shall have binding force on all authorities and persons throughout the Federal Republic of Nigeria". Section 1(3) of the Constitution provides that "If any other law is inconsistent with the provisions of this Constitution, this Constitution shall prevail, and that other law shall to the extent of the inconsistency be void".

Constitution of Nigeria.[109] The Police, having derived legitimacy from the laws of the Federal Republic of Nigeria, are according to the case of **Sambo v Nigeria Army Council**[110] "saddled with enormous responsibility of maintaining law and order in the society".

GENERAL POWERS OF THE NIGERIA POLICE

The powers of the police to maintain law and order in Nigeria has been extensively captured under chapter four, section 35 of the 1999 Constitution. Even though this section is fundamental human rights-based, nevertheless, the rights enumerated are not absolute; they are limited and qualified by the operations of the extant laws and the lawful acts of law enforcement agents (Police). The right to personal liberty under Nigerian law avails not only citizens, but even aliens. It can, however, be deprived in circumstances prescribed by any law in accordance with the Constitution[111]. Section 35[112] provides that:

1) Every person shall be entitled to his personal liberty and no person shall be deprived of such liberty save in the following cases and in accordance with a procedure permitted by law:-

   (a) in execution of the sentence or order of a court in respect of a criminal offence of which he has been found guilty;

   (b) by reason of his failure to comply with the order of a court or in order to secure the fulfilment of any obligation imposed upon him by law;

   (c) for the purpose of bringing him before a court in execution of the order of a court or upon reasonable suspicion of his having committed a criminal offence, or to such extent as may be reasonably necessary to prevent his committing a criminal offence;

   (d) in the case of a person who has not attained the age of eighteen years for the purpose of his education or welfare;

---

[109] This item 45, second Schedule, Part I of the 1999 Federal Republic of Nigeria Constitution provides that the Nigeria National Assembly comprising the Senate and the House of Representatives can exclusively make law to administer police and other government security services established by law.

[110] Sambo v Nigeria Army Council (2017)7NWLR, pt1565.

[111] Olomojobi, Yinka, Right to Personal Liberty in Nigeria (October 31, 2017). Available at SSRN: https://ssrn.com/abstract=3062580 or http://dx.doi.org/10.2139/ssrn.3062580

[112] Reproduced in full for emphasis.

(e) in the case of persons suffering from infectious or contagious disease, persons of unsound mind, persons addicted to drugs or alcohol or vagrants, for the purpose of their care or treatment or the protection of the community; or

(f) for the purpose of preventing the unlawful entry of any person into Nigeria or of effecting the expulsion, extradition or other lawful removal from Nigeria of any person or the taking of proceedings relating thereto:

Provided that a person who is charged with an offence and who has been detained in lawful custody awaiting trial shall not continue to be kept in such detention for a period longer than the maximum period of imprisonment prescribed for the offence.

(2) Any person who is arrested or detained shall have the right to remain silent or avoid answering any question until after consultation with a legal practitioner or any other person of his own choice.

(3) Any person who is arrested or detained shall be informed in writing within twenty-four hours (and in a language that he understands) of the facts and grounds for his arrest or detention.

(4) Any person who is arrested or detained in accordance with sub-section (1) (c) of this section shall be brought before a court of law within a reasonable time, and if he is not tried within a period of:-

(a) two months from the date of his arrest or detention in the case of a person who is in custody or is not entitled to bail; or

(b) three months from the date of his arrest or detention in the case of a person who has been released on bail, he shall (without prejudice to any further proceedings that may be brought against him) be released either unconditionally or upon such conditions as are reasonably necessary to ensure that he appears for trial at a later date.

(5) In sub-section (4) of this section, the expression "a reasonable time" means:-

(a) in the case of an arrest or detention in any place where there is a court of competent jurisdiction within a radius of forty kilometres, a period of one day; and

(b) in any other case, a period of two days or such longer period as in the circumstances that may be considered by the court to be reasonable.

(6) Any person who is unlawfully arrested or detained shall be entitled to compensation and public apology from the appropriate authority or person; and in this sub-section, "the appropriate authority or person" means an authority or person specified by law.

(7) Nothing in this section shall be construed:-

(a) in relation to sub-section (4) of this section, as applying in the case of a person arrested or detained upon reasonable suspicion of having committed a capital offence; and

(b) as invalidating any law by reason only that it authorises the detention for a period not exceeding three months of a member of the armed forces of the federation or a member of the Nigeria Police Force in execution of a sentence imposed by an officer of the armed forces of the Federation or of the Nigeria Police Force, in respect of an offence punishable by such detention of which he has been found guilty.

This provision is very instructive in regulating and balancing the sensitive duties of the police to carry out their job of crime detection, prevention and prosecution and the sacred obligation to protect and promote the fundamental rights and personal liberty of the citizens of Nigeria.

Section 4 of the Police Act provides for the duties of the Nigeria Police Force thus:-

> The police shall be employed for the prevention and detection of crime, the apprehension of offenders, the preservation of law and order, the protection of life and property and the due enforcement of all laws and regulations with which they are directly charged, and shall perform such military duties within or outside Nigeria as may be required of them by, or under the authority of this or any other Act.

These extensive duties are correlative of the power of the police and are at the heart of the whole social, cultural, economic and legal idea of policing. It has been held in the case of **Eze v IGP**[113] that "where the police properly act in the exercise of its power under section 4 of the Police Act, an arrest made therein cannot constitute a breach of fundamental rights". Consequently, where a citizen is arrested by the police in a legitimate exercise of their duty and on grounds of reasonable suspicion of having committed an offence, he cannot succeed in an action against the police for breach of fundamental human rights[114]. Generally, police officers are empowered to investigate allegations or complaints. They may take any action they deem fit to take upon investigation. They may arrest, detain and prosecute an alleged offender by virtue of section 4 of the Police Act and section 35 (1) (c) of the 1999 Constitution.[115] Corollary to this power of the police is also the power of citizens who have good reasons to make a report to the police about an offence so long as the citizen leaves the police to use their discretion in taking further steps.[116]

ENUGU STATE VAPP LAW (2019) AND THE POLICE POWER THEREIN

Primarily, it has been held in the case of **Odunayo v State**[117] that the police is the organ which carries out most investigations in the state. This is why it is important for any criminal justice law to create an extensive role for the police, without which the law may face dire enforceability challenges. The police have the duties of evidence preservation, fact finding and interrogation in cases of violence against women and girls under the Enugu State Violence Against Persons (Prohibition) Law (VAPP) (2019). Sections 28, 29 and 30 are dedicated to providing for the powers of the Police in administering and enforcing the Law. The relevant provisions are stated thus:

Section 28 provides that:

(1) A police officer at the scene of violence or that came to the scene as soon thereafter or as reasonably possible or to whom a report of violence has been made to shall have the duty of:

---

[113] Eze v I.G.P (2017) 4NWLR, Pt 1554.

[114] Okawo v C.O.P (2001) 1 CHR.

[115] Atakpa v Ebetor [2015]3 NWLR, pt 1447

[116] Ibid

[117] [2014] 12 NWLR, pt 1420

a. assisting a victim of violence to file the complaint regarding the violence;

b. Providing or arranging safe transport for the victim to an alternative residence, safe place or shelter where such is required;

c. Providing or arranging transportation for the victim to the nearest hospital or medical facility for treatment of injuries where such treatment is required;

d explaining to the victim his rights to protection against violence and remedies available in terms of this law;

e. explaining to the victim that he has the right to lodge a criminal complaint in addition to any remedy provided under this law;

f. accompanying the victim to the victim's place to collect personal belongings;

(2) Any police officer may, without an order from the court or warrant of arrest; arrest-

(a) any person whom he or she suspects upon reasonable grounds to have committed any offences under part 2; and

(b) any person against whom a complaint has been made for having committed any of the offences under part 2.

(3) A police officer in carrying out his or her duties under this law shall have the power:

(a) to remove or supervise the removal of a person from a shared residence where the court has issued such an order under this law;

(b) to remove or supervise the removal of any dangerous weapon used in other to commit an act of violence as contemplated in this law;

(c) to perform any other act considered necessary in other to insure the safety and well-being of the complainant.

This section is most instructive in enumerating the important duties to report and preserve evidence in a case of violence against women and girls. Section 28 (1) is in consonance with the ratio in the case of ***John Holt PLC V Allen***,[118]

[118] [2014] 17 NWLR, Pt. 1437.

where the court held that "a reasonable and genuine complaint made in good faith to the police that a crime had been committed cannot ground an action for malicious prosecution. The implication of this is that citizens are free to report cases of violence against women and girls without any fear of retribution. It is, therefore, the duty of the police according to the case of **Maduka v Ubah**[119] to investigate a report of commission of crime in the course of their statutory function of prevention, detection of crime and preservation of law and order.

Section 28(2) (a) and (b) provide for the power of the police officer to arrest any person who he reasonably suspects to have committed an offence of violence against women and girls. This section, coupled with the omnibus provision in section 28 (3) (c), empowers the police to gather evidence and interrogate the suspect as part of the police duty of preservation of law and order in the society.

Section 28 (3)(b) reinforces the power of the police to preserve evidence relating to the commission of offence of violence against women and children, the police can remove or supervise the removal of any dangerous weapon used in order to commit an act of violence as contemplated in this law. This important duty of the police has been predicated on the fact that evidence carries conviction and the police must procure and preserve evidence if they are to succeed in prosecuting offenders under the VAPP Law of Enugu state. The prosecutorial power of the police and the need for evidence is a constitutional provision. It has been held in the case of ***F.R.N v Martin***[120] that "by virtue of section 174(1) 1999 constitution, the police authority can prosecute any criminal suit either through its legally qualified officers or through any counsel they may engage for the purpose".

Section 29 of the VAPP Law of Enugu state provides that:

(1) whenever a court issues a protection order, the court shall make an order –

(a) authorizing the issue of warrant for the arrest of a respondent, in the prescribed form; and

---

[119] [2015] 11NWLR, Pt. 1470

[120] [2012] 14 NWLR. Pt 1320

(b) suspending the execution of such warrant subject to compliance with any prohibition, condition, obligation or order imposed in terms of section 26.

(2) The warrant referred to sub-section (1)(a) remains in force unless the protection order is set aside, or it is cancelled after execution.

(3) The registrar of the court shall issue the complaint with a second or further warrant of arrest, if the complaint files an affidavit in the prescribed form in which it is stated that such warrant is required for his protection and that the existing warrant of arrest has been

(a) executed or cancelled;

(b) lost or destroyed.

(4) A complaint may hand the warrant of arrest together with an affidavit in the prescribed form wherein it is stated that the respondent contravened any prohibition, condition, obligation or order contained in a protection order, to any police officer.

(5) If it appears to the police officer concerned that subject to sub-section (8), there are reasonable grounds to suspect that the complainant may suffer imminent harm as a result of the alleged breach of the protection order by the respondent, the police shall forthwith arrest respondent for allegedly committing the offence referred to in part 2.

(6) If the police officer concerned is of the opinion that there is sufficient ground in arresting the respondent in terms of paragraph (b) , he shall forthwith hand a written notice to the respondent which –

(a) specifies the name, the residential address and the occupation or status of the respondent;

(b) calls upon the respondent to appear before the court, and on the date and at the time specified in the notice, on a charge of committing the offence referred to in section 27(1) ; and

(c) contains a certificate signed by the police officer concerned to the effect that he handed the original notice to the respondent and he explained the import thereof to the respondent.

(7) The police officer shall forthwith forward a duplicate of original notice referred to in sub-section (6) to the registrar of the court concerned and the mere production in the court of such a duplicate

of original is *prima facie* proof that the original thereof was handed to the respondent specified therein;

(8) In considering whether or not the complainant may suffer imminent harm, as contemplated in sub-section (5), the police officer shall take into account;

(a) the risk to the safety or well-being of the complaint;

(b) the seriousness of the conduct comprising an alleged breach of the protection order; and

(c) the length of time since the alleged breach occurred.

(9) Whenever a warrant of arrest is handed to a police officer in terms of sub-section (4), the police officer shall inform the complainant of his right to simultaneously lay a criminal charge against the respondent, if applicable and explain to the complainant how to lay such charge.

Section 29 is most germane in providing for the procedure for the execution of warrant of arrest against offenders under the VAPP Law of Enugu State when the court has issued a protection order. The main purpose of this section is to calibrate the use of powers of arrest by the police. It is the law according to the case of ***I.G.P v Ikpila***[121] that "the enormous powers vested in the police do not give it the *carte blanche* to exercise powers with impunity or in reckless disregard and in contravention of the laws of the land".

Section 30 of the VAPP Law Enugu state provides thus:

(1) The court shall order a member of the Nigeria Police Force to seize any arm or dangerous weapon in the possession or under the control of the respondent if the court is satisfied on the evidence placed before it, including any affidavits supporting an application referred to section 25(1) above that:

(a) the respondent has threatened or expressed the intention to kill or injure himself or herself or any person in domestic relationship whether or not by means of such arm or dangerous weapon; or

[121] [2016] 9NWLR pt 1517.

(b) possession of such arm or dangerous weapon is not in the best interest of the respondent or any other person in a domestic relationship as a result of the respondent's

(i) state of mind or mental condition;

(ii) inclination to violence; or

(iii) use of or dependence on intoxicating liquor or drugs.

(2) Any arm seized in terms of sub-section (1) must be handed over to the Nigerian Police Force as contemplated in the Police Act Cap P19 Laws of the Federation of Nigeria, 2004 Firearms Act, Cap F28 Laws of the Federation of Nigeria, 2004.

(3) Any dangerous weapon seized in compliance with sub-section (1) above

(a) must be given a distinctive identification mark and retained in police custody for such period of time as the court shall determine; and

(b) shall only be returned to the respondent or, if the respondent is not the owner of the firearm or dangerous weapon, to the owner by the order of the court and on such condition as the court shall determine provided that the court is satisfied that it is in the interest of safety of any person concerned or in the public interest, the court shall order that the firearm or dangerous weapon be forfeited to the State.

Section 30 takes care of the duty of police to seize, receive and preserve evidence of weapon use in perpetrating violence against women and girls. This statutory provision buttresses the traditional duties of the police to handle and provide custody of weapon of violence used in the commission of crime. It can be argued that apart from the provision of section 30 which states that the court can order the police to carry out the duties of entering and seizing dangerous weapon from a respondent who upon reasonable grounds has been suspected to threaten or threatened violence upon the victim, the police has the discretion under the Police Act and other laws to carry out this duty *suo motu*. It has been held in the case of ***I.G.P v Ubah***[122] that:

[122] [2015] 11 NWLR pt 1471.

> There is no fixed or stipulated order of procedure for police investigation of crimes. Criminal investigations are carried out by the police based on the strength of the information at their disposal, the police investigator then uses his discretion to determine how to carry out the investigation.

CONCLUSION

The job of the police is the most sensitive one in the society. This is because they are entrusted with the sacred duty of preserving law and order in the society. With the rise in the violence against women and girls, also rises the burden on the police to take seriously their duties of crime detection, prevention and prosecution. The police should avoid wading into duties that would distract them, such as settlement of civil or commercial disputes. It has been held in the case of ***Iheanacho v N.P.F*** that "section 4 of the Police Act does not include the investigation or settlement of civil disputes or collection of debts'. The Nigeria Police should refrain from engaging in conduct that may bring disrepute to the Force, acts which are not limited to bribery and corruption, but also the consumption of alcohol on duty. In fact, the court has held in the case of ***Achuku v State***[123] that "the law does not take kindly to drinking alcohol by policemen on duty".

In the final analysis, the police, in order to effectively administer the VAPP Law in Enugu State, should desist from excessive and unreasonable use of force. The Supreme Court held in the case of ***Ononuju v State***[124] that "a trigger happy police force is not a good force. There is dire need for the training and retraining of the Nigeria Police Force if it is to take its place among the civilized police forces in the world".

---

[123] [2015] 6 NWLR pt 1456

[124] [2014] 8NWLR pt 1409

VIOLENCE AGAINST WOMEN: THE ROLE OF THE POLICE IN BUILDING CONFIDENCE AND PREVENTING THE RE-VICTIMISATION OF VICTIMS

By
Solo Akpanufot

Introduction

The notion that violence against women and girls is real and tangible has gained universal acceptability. In almost every society, at least one in five female populations have been physically, emotionally or sexually abused. In Nigeria, 25 per cent of women are said to have suffered various kinds of domestic violence. Prominent among such violence are battering, trafficking, rape and homicide (Moghalu, 2018). According to the European Institute for Gender Equality (EIGE, 2017), "Violence against women is the cause and result of structural inequalities experienced by women in many aspects of life — work, health, money, power, knowledge and time use — and remains the most brutal manifestation of gender inequality". Sadly, despite sustained global outcry against attacks on women and young girls, the practice, disappointingly, refuses to wane. The gap between efforts geared towards elimination of gender-Based violence and results achieved is yawning.

Violence against women, according to the Declaration on the Elimination of Violence Against Women, adopted by the United Nations General Assembly in 1993, is defined as "any act of gender-based violence that results in, or is likely to result in, physical, sexual, or psychological harm or suffering to women, including threats of such acts, coercion or arbitrary deprivation of liberty, whether occurring in public or private life" (UN, 1994). Nigeria is a signatory to the above UN declaration and has also adopted several national, sub-national and international standards against sexual and gender-based violence (SGBV). Government has also mainstreamed SGBV in her plans and policies with budgetary provisions for their implementation. Sadly, amidst all these efforts, abuse of women in the country has persistently remained an open sore. This widespread abuse manifests in many forms: Physical, Sexual, Economic and Psychological Violence. Often, these forms of violence are mutually inclusive and possess the capacity to re-inforce each other.

As a key pillar in the administration of criminal justice, the police are constitutionally authorised to exercise enormous, and sometimes meddling, powers on issues regarding violence against women. Police officers being "stewards of public trust", are empowered to "apply force and remove constitutional privileges when lawfully justified" (The Police Chief, 2006). All things being equal, police officers are the first actors who a victim of SGBV is most likely to approach for succour. Occupying the enviable position of first responders properly positions the police to play a critical role in enhancing the protection of the victim's safety and ensuring offender accountability. However, even with the power and resources available to the police, humanity increasingly witnesses low rate of prosecution and conviction of persons who assault women and girls, a phenomenon that has contributed immensely to exacerbating the incidence of SGBV globally. It is against this background that this paper seeks to discuss some conventional roles the police can play and suggest practical steps which could be taken to build confidence and prevent re-victimisation of victims.

Theoretical and Definitional Issues

The concept, "Violence Against Women" (VAW), is an evolving concept devoid of a universally acceptable definition. Variations in its definition keep increasing dramatically as many experts in the field get involved in the study (DeKeseredy and Schwartz, 2001; Jordan, 2004; Maier, 2014.). VAW prides itself as a key captivating social problem difficult to understand from a singular perspective of empirical and theoretical work. In this argument, two schools of thought emerged — the narrow definition school and broad definition school. Those on the narrow definition path focus primarily on physical abuse or sexual assaults involving penetration. They do not pay attention to other forms of abuses such as psychological, verbal, spiritual, and economic abuse. Proponents of this view argue that including psychological, verbal, spiritual, and economic harms with behaviours that hurt physically muddies "the water so much that it might be impossible to determine what causes abuse" (Gelles & Cornell, 1985, p. 23).

A second school of thought, with a broader view, believes it should cover areas of economic, psychological and emotional abuse. Their central argument is that "Psychological abuse can be just as, if not more, injurious than physical violence" (Adams, Sullivan, Bybee, & Greeson, 2008). These scholars are of the opinion that it is possible for most physical wounds to heal, but the damage to a woman's self-respect, dignity and ability to relate to others caused by emotional, verbal, and spiritual violence affects every aspect of her life and could last throughout her lifetime. For example, sexual assault to a woman goes beyond forced penetration, it encapsulates intentional/unsolicited touching, striking or causing of bodily injury in a sexual manner without a prior consent.

Most national, sub-national and international standards set up to eliminate abuse of women and girls see violence against women as a combination of both the broad and narrow perspectives advanced above. The UN Declaration on the Elimination of Violence Against Women defines VAW as :

> "Any act of gender-based violence that results in, or is likely to result in, physical, sexual, or psychological harm or suffering to women, including threats of such acts, coercion or arbitrary deprivation of liberty, whether occurring in public or private life".

The European Institute for Gender Equality (EIGE) emphasised that violence against women is rooted in historically unequal power relations between women and men, which leads to oppressive patterns of coercive control of men over women. It is the most pervasive gender inequality of our time, undermining women's dignity and integrity, and imposing serious harm on families, communities and societies (EIGE, 2017).

The Council of Europe Convention on preventing and combating violence against women and domestic violence, better known as the Istanbul Convention

(2011), defines violence against women from four key perspectives: physical, sexual, psychological and economic. Physical violence is explained as any act which causes "physical harm as a result of unlawful physical force. Physical violence can take the form of, among others, serious and minor assault, deprivation of liberty and manslaughter". Sexual violence depicts "Any sexual act performed on an individual without their consent. Sexual violence can take the form of rape or sexual assault". Psychological violence represents any act "which causes psychological harm to an individual". This can be seen in the form of coercion, defamation, verbal insult or harassment. Also, economic violence is that act or behaviour which causes "economic harm to an individual". Economic violence manifests in many dimensions such as "property damage, restricting access to financial resources, education or the labour market, or not complying with economic responsibilities, such as alimony".

According to Wikipedia, violence against women (VAW) in whatever form exists as a mechanism for "the subjugation of women, whether in society in general or in an interpersonal relationship". It is an act of violence committed primarily or exclusively "against women or girls". Such violence, as Wikipedia succinctly puts it, "may arise from a sense of entitlement, superiority, misogyny or similar attitudes in the perpetrator or his violent nature, especially against women" ("violence against women",n.d., para.2).

Violence against women persists not just because of the action or inaction of law enforcement officers but also because victims of such abuse lack the wherewithal to enforce their fundamental human rights. Most women condone various degrees of abuse for a number of reasons. Among these are "lack of income, the fear of losing child custody, low self-esteem, fear of stigmatization and much more" (Moghalu, 2018).Victims are often coerced to forgive the perpetrators while many are blamed for the offence (Maier, 2014). In a patriarchal society such as Nigeria, perceptions of rape and other gender-based violence are often pre-disposed to stereotype, bias and gender prejudice. The burden of proof hangs precariously on the neck of the victim. For her allegation to be believed, she must put her person on trial along with the offence committed against her. Perpetrators of rape, and sometimes with the connivance of law enforcement officers, will channel all arsenals within their disposal to discredit victim's allegation by discrediting her sexual reputation.

National, Sub-National and International Laws/Conventions on Violence Against Women and Girls

For effective enforcement of laws and policies relating to abuse of women and girls, it is imperative that police officers understand the existence of and how to enforce several standards put in place at national, sub-national and international levels to checkmate gender-based-violence. Acquainting themselves with these established standards is critical in the day to day policing, as knowledge gained thereof will considerably enhance adherence to the letters of the applicable laws and conventions.

Among the relevant laws, protocols and conventions on violence against women are:

i. African Charter on Democracy, Elections and Governance;
ii. Beijing Declaration and Platform for Action;
iii. Child Rights Act (CRA) 2003 which expands the horizons of human rights bestowed to citizens in Nigeria's 1999 constitution to children;
iv. Code of Conduct for Law Enforcement Officials;
v. Convention on the Elimination of all Forms of Discrimination against Women (CEDAW);
vi. Declaration on Basic Principles of Justice for Victims of Crime and Abuse of Power;
vii. Declaration on the Elimination of Violence against Women;
viii. ECOWAS protocol on good governance and Democracy;
ix. Police Act and Regulation CAP 359 LFN 1990;
x. The African Charter on Human and Peoples Rights and its Protocol on the Rights of Women in Africa;
xi. The Compulsory, Free, Universal Basic Education Act of 2004;
xii. The Constitution of the Federal Republic of Nigeria 1999 (as amended);
xiii. The Convention against Torture and other Cruel, Inhuman or Degrading Treatment or Punishment;
xiv. The Convention on the Rights of the Child;
xv. The International Covenant on Civil and Political Rights (ICCPR);
xvi. The International Covenant on Economic, Social and Cultural Rights (ICESCR):

xvii. The Nigeria Police Force Order;
xviii. The Violence against Persons (Prohibition) Act (VAPP) 2015;
xix. United Nations Basic Principles on the Use of Force and Firearms by Law Enforcement Officials;
xx. United Nations Code of Conduct for Law Enforcement Officers and;
xxi. United Nations Security Council Resolution 1325 on Women, Peace and Security.

Fundamental Human Rights

Fundamental Human Rights are captured in the relevant sections of Chapter IV of The Constitution of The Federal Republic of Nigeria 1999 (as amended). These include most of the rights adopted from the United Nations Universal Declaration of Human Rights:

i. Right to life (Section 33);
ii. Right to dignity of human persons (Section 34);
iii. Right to personal liberty (Section 35);
iv. Right to fair hearing (Section 36);
v. Right to Privacy (37);
vi. Right to freedom of thought, conscience and religion (Section 38);
vii. Right to freedom of expression and the press (Section 39);
viii. Right to peaceful assembly and association (Section 40);
ix. Right to freedom of movement (Section 41);
x. Right to freedom from discrimination (Section 42); and
xi. Right to acquire and own immovable property anywhere in Nigeria (Section 43).

Rights of Victims/Witnesses

Police officers who believe and consider their behaviour to be normal and acceptable by the public they serve must be able to recognise and respect rights of suspects, victims and witnesses in consonance with their fundamental rights. This observance is critical to effective and efficient policing. It will also aid the police to avoid unnecessary civil suits in violation of these rights (Balarabe, 2019). Among the rights of victims /witnesses are right:

i. To victim/witness information scheme

ii. To receive information on the date, time and location of the court hearing the trial
iii. To be given the opportunity to make a written statement to the court about how the crime has affected him/her
iv. To be informed to give evidence at a court and receive information that will help him prepare
v. To be protected from contact with the alleged offender at court, where possible
vi. Not to incriminate themselves while giving evidence
vii. Not to be harassed, even though this right is not found in the Constitution, nearly every Code has some type of rule forbidding harassing witnesses. This means that a lawyer conducting cross-examination cannot repeatedly ask same question, become hostile or threaten a witness
viii. To claim expenses incurred in process of giving evidence (Balarabe, 2019)

The Enugu State Violence Against Persons (Prohibition) Law, 2019 and Measurement of violence in the state.

In its effort to eliminate all forms of violence and discrimination against persons, protect victims of violence and punish offenders, the Enugu State government enacted the State's Violence Against Persons (Prohibition) Law 2019. This VAPP law came into effect on the 4th day of April, 2020. Prior to this Law, the state had enacted other laws to address infringements on the fundamental rights of its citizens. These previous laws are:

i. The prohibition of infringement of a widow's and widower's fundamental rights law, 2001 and;
ii. The Enugu State of Nigeria Anti-Discrimination Law 2008 No.2.

Offences covered in Part 2 of **The Enugu State Violence Against Persons (Prohibition) Law, 2019** are:

i. Rape
ii. Inflicting physical injury on a person
iii. Coercion

iv. Wilfully placing a person in fear of physical injury
v. Offensive conduct
vi. Female Circumcision or genital mutilation
vii. Forceful ejection from home.
viii. Economic abuse
ix. Forced isolation or separation from family and friends
x. Emotional, Verbal and Psychological abuse
xi. Harmful widowhood practice
xii. Abandonment of spouse, Children and other Dependant without sustenance
xiii. Stalking
xiv. Intimidation of a person
xv. Spousal/Partner battery
xvi. Harmful Traditional Practices
xvii. Substance Attack
xviii. Administering a substance with intent and
xix. Indecent Exposure

A cursory look at the above offences shows that they are not gender specific; however, greater number of women have fallen victims to most of the enumerated offences than men (WACOL, 2020). Therefore, if the Law is effectively implemented, the menace of violence against women and girls in the state will be reduced drastically.

One key factor that can help in achieving reduction in perpetration of the offences enumerated on the state's VAPP Law 2019 is accurate and comparable data on violence from across the 17 Local Government Areas (LGAs) in the State. This evidence-based data will go a long way to strengthen partnership between the police and key stakeholders, support advocacy efforts, help policy makers understand the dynamics of the problem and guide the design of interventions geared towards mitigating abuse of women and girls. In this regard, Women Aid Collective (WACOL) has set the ball rolling by consistently obtaining such data and analysing same for dissemination with key stakeholders. In this paper, we present below, analysis of data on Sexual and Gender-Based violations in Enugu State gotten within the 1st and 2nd quarter of the year 2020.

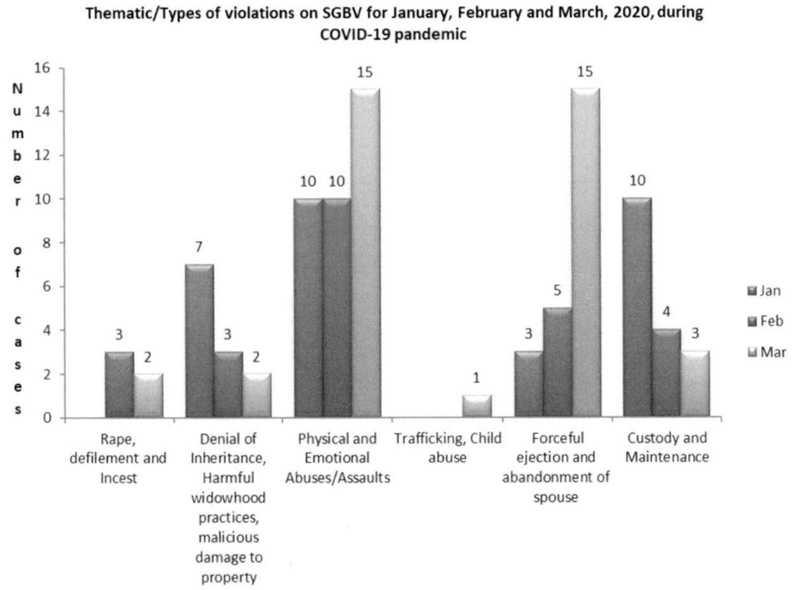

Figure 1:Women Aid Collective (WACOL) 2020. Summary of thematic or types of violations on SGBV for the first quarter of 2020, during COVID-19 pandemic. Enugu: WACOL.

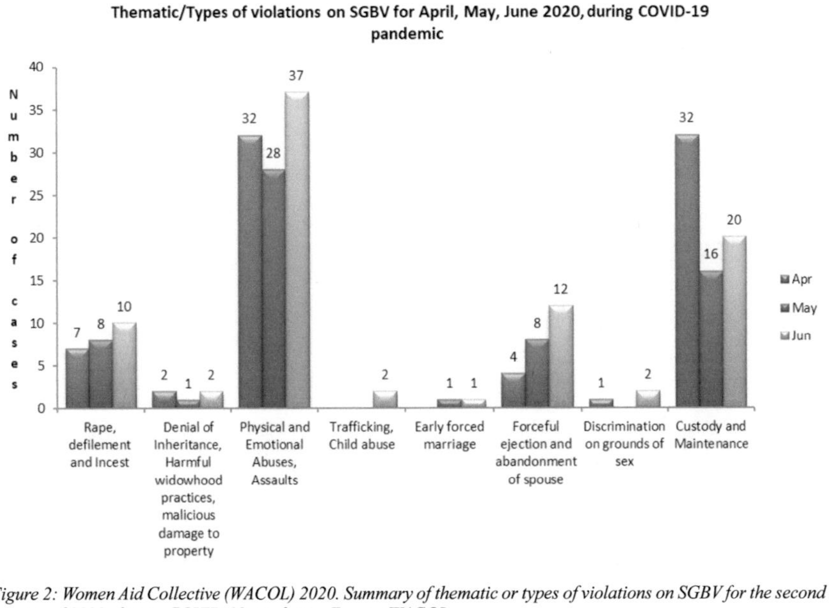

Figure 2: Women Aid Collective (WACOL) 2020. Summary of thematic or types of violations on SGBV for the second quarter of 2020, during COVID-19 pandemic. Enugu: WACOL.

From figures 1 and 2 above, it could be deduced that incidence of gender-based violence was higher in the 2nd Quarter of the year 2020 than it was in the first quarter. Physical and emotional abuses stood at 15 as the highest in the first quarter but rose with over 100 per cent increase (up to 37) in the 2nd quarter of the year. In both quarters, these forms of abuse were the highest reported cases. A total of 97 of such violent cases were reported between April, May and June 2020 while the reported data for January, February and March 2020 stood at 35. Aggregate reported cases of rape, defilement and incest were 5 in the 1st quarter of the year but rose astronomically to 26 in the 2nd quarter. In all, a total of 93 cases were reported against the 1st quarter while reported cases on SGBV in the 2nd quarter of the year stood at 227. One noticeable outcome of this analysis is that violence against women is on the rise during the Covid-19 pandemic. Consequently, government and the police have to be on red alert to flatten the curve of this ugly trend in the state.

The role of Police in building confidence and preventing the re-victimisation of victims.

The police could achieve much success in the quest to eradicate Gender-Based Violence if they adhere strictly to Police Ethics and Code of Conduct in the discharge of their constitutionally assigned responsibilities. Knowledge of and respect to various legal instruments upon which the police derive their very authority is critical in modern day policing. The powers and responsibilities of the Police are set out under the Police Act (Cap. P.19) Laws of the Federation of Nigeria, 2004. In section 4 thereof, the following duties are assigned to the Nigeria Police Force:

i. Prevention and detection of crime;
ii. The preservation of law and order;
iii. Apprehension and prosecution of offenders;
iv. Due enforcement of all laws and regulations with which they are directly charged;
v. Perform such military duties within or without Nigeria as may be required by them by, or under the authority of this or any other Act; and
vi. Protection of life and property.

According to Ojukwu (2016),

> "Police service delivery is to be seen in terms of her ability to constantly and consistently meet the expectations of her customers. This is not the responsibility of the high command alone. All personnel should be involved in this drive if the organization is to remain relevant. This drive entails consultation, preventive tactics, and timeliness in response to distress calls, quick and efficient disposal of allocated cases. It also embraces commitment, openness, accessibility and availability, as well as courtesy, fairness, and friendliness".

It is important to note that as law enforcement officers constitutionally empowered to exercise a great level of authority on the people, police officers' conduct, openly or secretly, must always be guided by their professional ethics and in consonance with relevant provisions of the constitution. As Ojukwu (2016) rightly observed, the fundamental duty of a police officer is:

> "To serve mankind; to safeguard lives and property; to protect the innocent against deception, the weak against oppression or intimidation, and the peaceful against violence or disorder; and to respect the constitutional rights of all persons to liberty, equality and justice".

As first responders and gate keepers in the arena of criminal justice, the police are strategically positioned to play critical role in building confidence of victims, safeguarding their protection against re-victimisation and enhancing offender accountability. The way and manner police play this crucial role directly affects victim's willingness to engage in the criminal justice process and by extension, the likelihood of decreasing/eliminating incidences of violence against women and girls.

The paper primarily examines the role of the police in line with the established Code of Ethics for Law Enforcement. It posits that if the police can discharge their duties effectively and efficiently in line with established code of ethics for law enforcement and various national, sub-national and international standards, the menace of gender-based violence will be reduced to the barest minimum in our society. The paper examines these roles under the following headings:

A. Strict observance of the Rule of Law

The work has advanced the argument that the police remain the first point of call for a victim of abuse. The police are the victim's first contact with the criminal justice system. It is expected that as an officer of the law, a police officer who investigates the suspected wrongdoing and makes an arrest should do so in accordance with the law. Put differently, the rights of victims, suspects and witnesses must be respected in effective policing. The cardinal underpinning of the rule of law stipulates that:

> The Law prevails and superintends over the will of man, group or institutions; and no man is a law unto himself, as the law has common applicability" (Ojukwu, 2016).

Where an investigative police officer fails to observe the Rule of Law, he is likely to do injustice to either or all the parties involved. Again, this lapse in service delivery has far- reaching implications for the police as an institution. As Balarabe (2019) observed, police officers who believe and consider their behaviour to be normal and acceptable by the public they serve must be able to recognise and observe rights of suspects, victims and witnesses in consonance with their fundamental rights for effective and efficient service delivery. Any act to the contrary may result into civil suits against the police in violation of these rights.

B. Confidentiality in dealing with victims

In dealing with victims of abuse, a police officer is expected to do so with utmost privacy and even secrecy as a crucial component of a victim's safety. Whatever a police officer sees, hears and learns in the course of duty is expected to be kept secret. Secrecy is a universal code of conduct for law enforcement officers. Sensitive information of victims, when exposed, leaves survivors in danger. It will also trigger victims not to report cases of abuse to the police nor seek for help from any source. The resultant effect may be cataclysmic to the victims and her relatives.

The Police Regulations 370(b) (First Schedule) of CAP 359 LFN 1990 sees this unprofessional act as a "breach of confidence". In Section 1(1) of the official secrets Act, CAP 335 LFN 1990 it is stated that:

> A person who (a) transmits any classified matter to a person to whom he is not authorised on behalf of the government to transmit it; or (b) obtains, reproduces or retains any classified matter which he is authorised on behalf of the government to obtain, reproduce or retain, as the case may be, shall be guilty of an offence.

Above presupposes that personal history and identity of victims of violent abuse are to be treated confidentially. Anything to the contrary is an offence under the law. Only on a need-to-know or need-to-share basis should a police officer reveal such secrets. Once a victim is assured that her matter would be treated with utmost confidentiality and that no harm would come to her and no other person would hear about her case except she want it, the victim will be obliged to open up and seek redress/support.

C. Effective Partnership and Collaborations with policing actors.

To properly address incidences of violence against women, Moghalu, (2018) has advanced the imperativeness of joining forces with other violence-focused organisations or women's platforms to raise awareness on the issue. Partnership and collaboration with critical policing actors, governmental and non-governmental institutions as well as development partners is critical in supporting law enforcement officers to effectively police our communities and bring about a reduction in the prevalence of SGBV. When the police choose to work in silos, they deny themselves of requisite support from other organisations.

Furthermore, the police as an institution established by law, must be receptive to checks and balances brought about by the establishment of police oversight bodies. Civilian oversight bodies such as the National Human Rights Commission, Police Service Commission, National Assembly committees on Police Affairs, Ministry of Police Affairs, etc must be seen as partners in progress and nothing more. These bodies help significantly in policing the police, checking excesses of recalcitrant police officers especially in view of the rising citizens' concerns about excessive use of force by some police officers and their vulnerability to abuse of statutory power.

D. Sustained training/re-training, monitoring and mentoring support to junior officers by senior police officers

All police officers need sustained training, monitoring and mentoring as regards how best they can deal with matters pertaining to gender-based violence. Officers should be trained to be more sensitive to women's feelings concerning violence. Application and statement from victims should be handled, not at the counter by untrained officers, but by an officer who is well-schooled on family violence and gender issues. Most untrained officers often persuade the parties to make peace. They fail to see violence against women as a crime that the police should handle. Often women who are victims of violence are handled as perpetrators.

E. Proper investigation of offences, prosecution of offenders and wide publication of perpetrators.

Police officers should swiftly investigate cases of violence against women, arrest and diligently prosecute such perpetrators.

The conviction to correctional centres or imposition of stringent fines on the perpetrators must be given wide publicity in order to serve as deterrence to those who may have such violent tendencies. Furthermore, the police should create and maintain registers of offenders. Names of perpetrators sentenced to correctional centres or made to pay stringent fines should be properly documented in the register and published in places like the court, police station, offenders residences or hometown, churches, mosques, markets, schools, clubs, newspapers etc. When this is done, young boys with inclination to commit such violent acts will see the need to retrace their steps.

F. Reduction of response time to distress call

As a matter of priority, the police should make effort to reduce their response time to distress calls and act professionally when doing so to avoid victimisation of innocent person or persons. It is also important to put in place a system that will support victims of crime to spend little or nothing in the pursuit of justice as most victims are economically disadvantaged citizens.

G. Creation and strengthening of special sections/units in all police formations to handle issues relating to SGBV

It is also important that the police create and empower special sections or units within the police with a mandate to handle issues concerning women, children and other vulnerable persons in the society. Personnel of such units should be trained on their job specifications and retained for a long time before they can be transferred to other sections to enable their knowledge gain traction and impact on the system. In this case, Juvenile Welfare Centre (JWC), Family Support Unit (FSU) and Gender Unit (GU) need to be established and supported to function optimally across all divisions and police formations.

H. Re-invigoration of Police Accountability Unit

Accountability units of the police should be re-invigorated to support the fight against unprofessional conduct by the personnel across board. Mechanism for processing public complaints needs to be established and strengthened to speed up the process of deepening professionalism within the police.

The police should also interface with and sensitise community members on how to check police professional conduct while lawfully resisting impunity. This will go a long way in improving police service delivery and its responsiveness to issues of gender-based violence.

I. Impartiality in handling of cases of SGBV

The police are saddled with the task of relieving and helping SGBV victims by guiding them to the path of recovery, as well as arresting and prosecuting the offenders. It is important that in doing these, officers should be seen to be impartial in all ramifications. Cases where police officers try to mend the relationship of both parties by forcing the victims to collect money from the offenders, in order to forget about the case, constitute high level of professional misconduct and is against the principle of impartiality.

In dealing with cases of sexual abuse, it is imperative that the police build confidence of the victim, show empathy towards her and display no pity on the offender irrespective of the relationship between both parties. Anything to the contrary will re-enforce the resolve of the offender to re-commit the crime while the victim is left in total bewilderment regretting why she ever reported the case to the police in the first place.

J. Helping Victims to Access Medical Care and Awareness Creation on SGBV

It is important that victims of rape or sexual violation should be supported by the police to receive adequate medical attention. The Investigating Police Officer (IPO) should also communicate the medical facility on the importance of the case. The medical unit of the police should be supported to organise medical outreaches in communities as part of its Corporate Social Responsibility (CSR). Relevant units of the police can unite to carry out town hall meetings, public sensitisation and enlightenment campaigns on the dangers of SGBV and how the victim could reach out to the police for support. The police need to deepen proactive as against reactive policing which majority of police officers are currently practicing.

K. Institutionalisation of functional reward and recognition systems

As part of the institutional human resource management function, the police should institutionalise a functional system to reward performance and motivate officers who have demonstrated exceptional behaviour in the discharge of their duties. This will aid significantly in improving officers' attitudes, practice, behaviour and performance. In this respect, the paper strictly recommends non-financial rewards such as awards/recognition, promotion, participation in professional trainings and increased job responsibilities. Such awards as "most gender friendly officer of the year", "community policing compliance award", "excellence performance award", "best investigative police officer (IPO) of the year award" etc can go a long way in triggering compliance to established code of ethics for law enforcement among police officers leading to a re-positioning of the police for better policing.

Conclusion

Victims of violence against women most often suffer physically, psychologically, emotionally and economically. In some instances, the trauma and pains they go through could force some to lose their minds and attempt suicide. Many victims suffer some level of vulnerability and there are instances where even some prosecuting police officers handling these cases capitalise on this vulnerability to perpetrate professional misconduct against the victims. Acting against the established code of conduct for law enforcement officers as explained above are the bane of policing in Nigeria. Again, this could be blamed on the amorality and lack of civility in Nigeria's public institutions. The earlier these negative tendencies are nipped in the bud, the more successful our quest to eliminate violence against women and girls will become.

A time has come for the police to approach policing within the boundaries of tolerable conduct. Laws addressing gender-based violence such as **The Enugu State Violence Against Persons (Prohibition) Law, 2019** must be enforced professionally without undue drama and bias. As enlightened people living in a civilised dispensation, we must mobilise ourselves to de-mobilise men with tendencies to abuse women and girls in any form. The role of the police becomes increasingly important if we must put an end to victim's re-victimisation and guarantee their safety in the life after violations.

REFERENCES

Adams, A.E., Sullivan, C.M., Bybee, D., & Greeson, M.R. (2008). Development of the scale of economic abuse. *Violence Against Women*, 15, 563-588.

Council of Europe (2011). Convention on Preventing and Combating Violence against Women and Domestic Violence, Council of Europe Treaty Series No. 210, Date: 11.05.2011, Istanbul.

Declaration on the elimination of violence against women. New York, United Nations, 23 February 1994 (Resolution No. A/RES/48/104).

DeKeseredy, W.S., Schwartz, M.D., Fagen, D., & Hall, M. (2006). Separation/divorce sexual assault: The contribution of male peer support. Feminist Criminology, 1, 228-250.

Gelles, R.J., & Cornell, C.P. (1985). *Intimate violence in families*. Beverly Hills: Sage.

Jordan, J. (2004). *The word of a woman? Police, rape and belief.* New York: Palgrave Macmillan.

Maier, S. L. (2014). *Rape, victims and investigations*. Experiences and perceptions of law enforcement officers responding to reported rapes: Routledge.

Meg.Townsend et.al (2005). Law Enforcement Response to Emergency Domestic Violence Calls for Service.

Moghalu Kingsley (2008). Build, Innovate and Grow: My vision for my country. Ibadan: Bookcraft.

Ojukwu, Emmanuel C.S. (2016). Discovering the Police: an excursion into thepolice personality, powers, performance, and prudence. Ibadan: Craft Books Limited.

"Recommendations of the Committee of Ministers to member states on the protection of women against violence" (PDF). *Council of Europe Committee of Ministers. 30 April 2002.*

Suleiman, Balarabe (2019). Mainstreaming Fundamental Human Rights, Rights of Suspects, Victims and Witnesses in Service Delivery. A paper presented at a 2-day workshop Sensitization Workshop on Community

Oriented Policing (CoP) organized for Area Commanders, Divisional Police Officers and Senior Officers of other Policing Agencies held at The State Police Headquarters, Enugu State Command and facilitated by the Nigeria Policing Programme (NPP). Tuesday 16th and Wednesday 17th July 2019.

The European Institute for Gender Equality (EIGE) Gender Equality Index 2017: Measurement framework of violence against women -Report.

The Police Chief, Vol.73, No.11, November 2006.

Violence against women. (2020, September 14). In *Wikipedia*. Retrieved from https://en.wikipedia.org/wiki/Violence_against_women.

Women Aid Collective (WACOL), 2020. Summary of thematic or types of violations on SGBV for the first and second quarter of 2020, during COVID-19 pandemic.Enugu: WACOL.

Zoe McKee, Katrin Mueller-Johnson & Heather Strang (2020). Impact of a Training Programme on Police Attitudes Towards Victims of Rape: a Randomised Controlled Trial. *Cambridge Journal of Evidence-Based Policing* volume 4, pages39 – 55 (2020).

MOVING FORWARD: ADDRESSING THE GAPS WITHIN THE ENUGU STATE VAPP LAW (2019) AND VAPP ACT (2015)

By
Obinna James Edeh (LLM, LLB, BL)

Department of Public Law
Faculty of Law
University of Nigeria

Abstract

One of the major benefits of democratisation is the recognition that the human rights of citizens must be respected, protected and promoted. There cannot be a democratic process if the government does not assume and execute this tripartite duty with diligence. This is more so, where the State is a signatory to various international legal documents that commit them to protect the rights of their citizens, particularly the vulnerable persons. In recognition of this responsibility, the Nigerian government signed into law the Violence Against Persons Prohibition Law (2015). Various States in Nigeria, including Enugu State, has also adopted similar provisions and re-enacted them, hence, the Enugu State Violence Against Persons Prohibition Law (2019). However, since the adoption of this law at the national and state levels, the expectation that violence, particularly against women and girls would become history, has began to diminish. The law has also become what Bentham called a "bawling on paper". More worrisome is the fact that there are gaps within the law that could hinder the effective protection which it made to confer on vulnerable persons in Nigeria. Therefore, this paper will place the law side by side with international and national human rights instruments relative to women and girls to see how to bring it at par with global norms and strengthen the effectiveness of its implementation.

Introduction

The Violence Against Persons Prohibition Act (2015) is the most comprehensive legislative document in Nigeria to criminalise Sexual and Gender-Based Violence (SGBV).[125] The enactment of the Act in 2015 followed the high incidence of violence visited on vulnerable persons within public and domestic settings. The Act was the first to recognise that violence comes in different categories and thus, specified punishment for each act of violence or attempt to commit that act. The VAPP Act, as well as the VAPP Laws of the various states, including Enugu State, condemned and punishes physical[126] and psychological violence[127] against a person and against a person's property[128], which hitherto has not been so recognised by any legal

[125] Comprising 48 sections and 6 forms, The Act applies to the Federal Capital Territory. However, same version of the VAPP Act has been reenacted by various states in Nigeria, including Enugu State VAPP Law (2019),

[126] Section 5 of the Enugu State VAPP Law (2019) provides that any person who wilfully causes or inflicts physical injury on another person by means of any weapon, substance or object, commits an offence and is liable, on conviction to an imprisonment not exceeding five years or both or a fine not exceeding N100,000 or to both fine and imprisonment. This is a replication of the provisions of Section 2 (1) of the VAPP Act (2015). By Sub (2), anyone who attempts to commit such offence is liable on conviction to imprisonment for a term not exceeding five years or to a fine not exceeding N50,000 or both, Sub Section (2) of the VAPP Act curiously, provides that an attempt to commit this offence attracts a sentence of three years imprisonment or a fine of N200,000 or both. As would be seen in later pages, this paper believes that the punishments prescribed by the VAPP Act and Laws appears to be a slap on the wrist and may not be sufficient to deter occurrence and re-occurrence of violence.

[127] Section 13 of the Enugu State VAPP Law (2019)

[128] Section 11 of the VAPP Act (2015) prescribes a punishment of N300,000 or a term of two years imprisonment or both on anyone who damages the property of another with intent to cause annoyance or distress to the victim; attempting to commit the offence attracts a fine of N200,000 or one year imprisonment or both.

document in Nigeria.[129] For instance, the offence of forced isolation and separation from family[130], forceful ejection from the home,[131] female genital circumcision or mutilation[132], emotional, verbal and psychological abuse,[133] harmful widowhood practices,[134] stalking,[135] spousal battery,[136] harmful traditional practices[137] and indecent exposure[138] are some of the offences which, hitherto, were not existing or scattered in different documents.

Furthermore, the VAPP Act (2015) took a different approach in defining violence, moving from a restrictive point of view to a more liberal perspective, as recommended by regional and international human rights laws. The most important benefit of this approach is that it offers more protection to vulnerable persons[139] who have suffered injuries without any form of remedy. Furthermore, noting the increasing level of sexual crime in Nigeria, the Act made broad provisions for different acts that constitutes sexual offences and expanded the elements of these offences. For instance, section 1 of the Act provides that an offence of rape is complete if a person intentionally penetrates the vagina, anus or mouth of another person with any other part of his or her body or anything else. This broad definition is laudable because it recognises that rape is not a gender-specific offence; but can be committed by anyone who performs any of the actions stated therein. The Act commendably increased the punishment for rape to life imprisonment; except where the offender is less than 14 years, in which case, term of 14 years shall be imposed. It also

---

129 Section 290 of the Criminal Code provides that a person in peaceable possession of property has the right to such reasonable force to defend his possession of the property against everyone else, provided he causes no physical harm to the trespasser. A similar provision can be found in sections 291 and 292 of the Code. However, the VAPP Act/Law takes this further by prohibiting malicious damage to property and prescribing punishments for such actions.

130 Section 13 of the VAPP Act (2015)

131 Section 8

132 Section 6

133 Section 14

134 Section 15

135 Section 17

136 Section 19

137 Section 20

138 Section 26

139 Section 46 of the Act lists vulnerable groups as comprising: women, children, persons living under extreme poverty, persons with disability, the sick, the elderly, ethnic and religious minority groups, refugees, internally displaced person, migrants and persons in detention.

prohibited and provided stringent punishment for gang rape as the offenders would be liable to serve for 20 years imprisonment without an option of fine. However, it is the view of this paper that the term should be increased to life imprisonment as there is no clear difference between the actions of a sole rapist and gang rapists.

Despite the innovations and laudable provisions of the Act, and the various VAPP Laws across states, a close study of the provisions indicates that they still fall short of international and regional human rights laws which Nigeria has adopted and ratified. In terms of practicality, the Act did not address some urgent substantive and procedural issues that exacerbate and perpetuate, particularly, violence against women and girls in Nigeria. To this end, this paper would identify these provisions, use them to highlight the loopholes and shortcomings of the Act and then recommend that a stronger legal regime is absolutely necessary to protect women and girls from violence in the country.

The paper is divided into five sections, comprising the present introductory section; a brief analysis of selected international and domestic legal frameworks existing prior to the enactment of the Violence Against Persons Prohibitions Act; a review of the existing gaps in the law; and a section on summary and conclusion. The objective of this paper is to identify the lacuna within the Act which may affect the implementation of the provisions across states and the Federal Capital Territory and make recommendations to close the gaps and strengthen the protection of vulnerable persons from violence.

International and Regional Legal Instruments for the Prevention of Violence Against Women

a) The International Convention on the Elimination of all forms of Discrimination Against women (CEDAW)

This is the most specific but comprehensive international document to protect women from discrimination and harmful traditional practices.[140] CEDAW

[140] Article 1 of the Convention defines discrimination against women to include any distinction, exclusion, or restriction, made on the basis of sex which has the effect or purpose of impairing or nullifying the recognition, enjoyment, or exercise by women, irrespective of their marital status, on the basis of equality with men and women, of human rights and fundamental freedoms in the political, economic, social, cultural, civil or any other field.

was adopted in 1979 and has been ratified by over a hundred countries, including Nigeria.[141] As the name implies, the Convention prohibits all forms of discrimination and not violence against women. However, there is no gainsaying that acts of discrimination could predispose women to violence of different forms. For instance, unequal pay, disinheritance of the female gender, negative widowhood practices, are acts that give rise to mental, psychological and sometimes, physical violence. Therefore, this paper argues that the Violence Against Persons Act/Law must recognise that acts of discrimination against women, which predispose them to violence, and an amended VAPP Law should criminalise all acts of discrimination directed at women and girls. Domesticating the provisions of the CEDAW, in line with Section 12 of the 1999 Constitution (as amended), is the best place to start towards recognising the fact that discrimination of women is a form of violence against women. If the CEDAW is domesticated, it would be easier to make a case to include discrimination as an act of violence in the VAPP Act/Laws across Nigeria.

b) The African Charter on Human and Peoples Rights (Banjul Charter 1981)

Nigeria has signed up to and equally domesticated the African Charter on Human and Peoples Rights, otherwise known as the Banjul Charter 1981. The Charter makes comprehensive prohibitions to protect citizens of member states from any actual or threatened act that violate or threaten to violate their human rights.[142] Pursuant to the African Charter on Human and Peoples Right (Enforcement and Ratification) Act, the rights provided in the document apply directly in Nigeria as if it were a local legislation. Most of the rights therein are same as those in the constitution, but unlike the constitution, it is not subject to claw back clauses or modifications which the constitution might

[141] To underscore the comprehensive nature of the Convention in relation to the rights of women, see : 'A Factsheet on CEDAW: Treaty for the Rights of Women' ; Amnesty International: https://www.amnestyusa.org/files/pdfs/cedaw_fact_sheet.pdf accessed September, 15, 2020

[142] Having been domesticated pursuant to Section 12 of the 1979, now 1999 Nigerian Constitution vide the African Charter on Human and Peoples Rights (Ratification and Enforcement) Act, Cap. A 9, LFN 2004, the rights provided therein can be locally applied in Nigeria. Article 5 of the Act guarantees the inherent right to dignity and prohibits all forms of exploitation, degradation in the form of slavery, slave trade, torture, cruel inhuman or degrading punishment and treatment

suffer in the event of national emergency.[143] Furthermore, the Charter has added a protocol which specifically protects and promotes the rights specific to women in Africa.

c) Protocol to the African Charter on Human and Peoples Rights on the Rights of Women in Africa

Simply known as the Maputo Protocol, it was adopted in Mozambique on the 11th of July 2003. In terms of broad definition and specificity to women's right, this is the most detailed legislation at the regional level that seeks to eliminate all forms of violence against women within the continent.[144] Various scholars have hailed the adoption of the protocol, declaring it as one with potential to galvanise a regional response to the incidence of violence against women. The adoption of the Protocol has also inspired the enactment of specific laws in several countries in Africa to protect women from violence. For instance, the provisions of the Protocol led to the adoption of the family code on gender equality which prohibits polygamy and affords children equal access to fundamental rights, irrespective of status and gender in Benin Republic. The Convention also inspired the Customary Marriage and Divorce Act in Sierra Leone which protects women who chose to enter customary marriage from forced marriages. It was the basis for the Promotion of Equality and Prevention of Unfair Discrimination Act in South Africa.[145]

Indeed, most of the provisions of the Violence Against Persons Prohibitions Law were drafted in line with the Protocol. Article 1 of the Protocol broadly defines violence against women to include any act that causes or is likely

---

143 In Abacha v. Fawehinmi (2000) 6 NWLR (Pt. 660) 228; the Supreme Court acknowledged that by virtue of its enactment as a Nigerian law, it has a binding force and, yet being an international convention, does not fall under the laws that are affected by the Constitution (Suspension and Modification) Decree 1993

144 According to the Women, Gender and Development Directorate of the African Union Commission, the Maputo Protocol is one of the most comprehensive set of human rights for African women; https://au.int/sites/default/files/documents/31520-doc-maputo protocol on womens rights a living document for womens human rights in africa submitted by the women gender and development directorate wgdd of the african union commission.pdf Accessed September 15, 2020

145 'Maputo Protocol on Women's Rights: A Living Document for Women's Human Rights in Africa' (2016) ; A report presented on the 'State of Ratification of the Maputo Protocol' on the margins of the UN Commission on the Status of Women in New York; cited in Ibid page 1.

to cause, physical, sexual, psychological and economic harm including the threat of such harm to a woman. Section 2 of the Enugu State VAPP Law (2019) also defines 'violence' in the same way; both laws include provisions which enumerate the type of violence that is prohibited against non-state actors to include: wrongful arrest or detention, assault, use of force without lawful authority, unlawful entry into premises and demolition of property without due process. As laudable as this provision appears, it is curious as to why the provision is limited to acts committed only by non-state actors. The clear interpretation is that when such acts are committed by state actors, the VAPP Law cannot intervene to protect the victim even if the action was done extra-judicially. Therefore, this paper argues that section must be amended to prohibit state and non-state actors from committing any of the violative acts stated in that provision. This is best way to assure protection for the vulnerable in the society, especially women and girls.

Article 4 of the Protocol mandates State Parties to respect the integrity and security of the person and take further measures to enact laws to prohibit all forms of Violence Against Women including forced labour. The State Parties are to adopt political, administrative and legal measures to ensure the prevention, punishment and eradication of all forms of violence against women among others. There is no gainsaying that the enactment of the VAPP Act/Law is a step towards implementing the provisions of this treaty although the VAPP Act and Laws are not restricted to the feminine gender.

One of the flaws of the Protocol is its clear inability to hold states accountable for failing to protect women and prevent violence meted out to women and girls. The African Commission on Human and Peoples Rights have repeatedly held that states that adopt the regional conventions have a responsibility to protect women from any form of violence from a third party irrespective of whether the violator is a public or private person. According to the Commission in the *Egyptian Initiative for Person Rights and INTERRIGHTS v. the Government of Egypt*, state parties can be held vicariously liable for any violation of the rights or violence against women if it did not exercise due diligence towards preventing such act.[146] Thus, despite the enactment of the VAPP Act/Law, this paper argues that in future amendments, a similar obligation should be taken

[146] Interights v. Egypt, Comm. 312/2005, 21st ACHPR AAR Annex II (2006-2007)

up by the state to take positive measures towards preventing and ending all forms of violence against women and girls.

Domestic Framework

a) The 1999 Constitution of the Federal Republic of Nigeria (as amended)

The first and most important domestic instrument for the protection of women and girls from violence is the Nigerian constitution. Chapter IV therein reaffirms Nigeria's commitment towards protecting the rights of her citizens. The constitutional provisions clearly prohibit all acts of violence from individuals, groups or state agents except as permitted and within the limits allowed by constitution or any other law in force. Thus, section 33 of the constitution provides that no one shall be deprived of his life except in the manner provided by law. Therefore, any act of violence which leads to death clearly infringes this provision of the constitution.[147] Section 34 (1) grants to every Nigerian the freedom from all acts that are degrading or inhuman.[148] Further, the section protects the dignity of the person and makes it clear that no one shall be subjected to any act of torture, slavery, servitude, forced or compulsory labour in any form.

Flowing from the above piece of legislation, women and girls in Nigeria are protected from any act of torture, slavery and servitude as well as forced or compulsory labour. There are questions as to whether this provision protects from other acts of violence not specifically mentioned in the constitution.

---

[147] Usman Kaza v. The State; SC. 21.2/2004 delivered 15th day of February 2008. The Court held *inter alia* that it would be a dangerous precedent if individuals are authorised to take the law into their hands as the appellant in this case. The Court per Mohammad (JSC) as he then was, reiterated that Sharia guarantees and values the sanctity and dignity of human life. Thus, Nigerian law outlaws unlawful taking of human life.

[148] The point must be made here that the Supreme Court has held that the imposition of the sentence of death in deserving cases cannot be violative of the right to human dignity or termed an inhuman or degrading treatment. See Kalu v. The State (1988) 13 NWLR (PT. 583) 531. The case is the *locus classicus* on the definition and contours of the right to human dignity in Nigeria. The Supreme Court in *Uzoukwu V. Ezeonu II (1991)* 6 NWLR noted that Inhuman treatment is any treatment which is barbarous, uncouth and cruel treatment. It is a treatment which has no human feeling on the part of the person inflicting the barbarity or cruelty

Considering that the express mention of a thing indicates the exclusion of the other, it could be said that the constitution is restrictive as to the protection it confers on Nigerians, especially women, from violence. It cannot be gainsaid that torture, by definition of the United Nations Convention Against Torture (UNCAT), implies mental or psychological harm, this definition cannot be validly stretched to include economic violence, verbal abuse as well as some harmful traditional practices visited on women and girls which cannot be infused under the definition of torture. Indeed, the courts would hesitate to extend beyond what the law anticipates, see *Uzoukwu v. Ezeonu II.*[149]

One of the major challenges that attends using constitutional provisions to protect women from violence in that the obligation therein are couched in negative language. Therefore, the law does not give government the responsibility to take any action towards the protection of citizens (women and girls) from violence. The obligations are reactionary and therefore not sufficient to protect the rights of women and girls from violence. The international and regional commitments freely entered by Nigeria mandates it to ensure that citizens enjoy the full protection of their human rights. Therefore, conformity to these provisions implies that a legal regime imposing positive obligations should be enacted by the state.

b) The Criminal Law:

Prior to the enactment of the Violence Against Persons Prohibition Act (2015), the Nigerian Criminal Law, comprising the Criminal Code and the Penal Code, were the major national laws protecting women from aggression and violence. The question would be why did the enactment of the VAPP become necessary in the face of the existing criminal laws? The first reason is that most of the provisions of the criminal law that are specific to women and girls provide for only offences that relate to sexual abuse. Other grievous acts of violence such as verbal, psychological, mental and economic abuse, were not fully treated by the criminal code. Furthermore, because of the herculean procedure for amending the criminal code, most of the penalties stated therein have become obsolete and ridiculous. Again, as society develops, new forms

[149] (1991) 6 NWLR (Pt. 200) 708 The court held that no court or tribunal has the powers to go outside or beyond the definitions and categories expressly mentioned in the constitution to add other forms of violation.

of violence are meted out on women, and thus, it was necessary to have a legal regime that addresses and punishes such acts. Finally, the Violence Against Persons Prohibition Act and Law makes provision for protecting the victim when there is a reasonable suspicion that she might be violated. These provisions are geared to ensure that the threat of violence are nipped in the bud before it is manifested.

The criminal code which operates in the southern part of Nigeria provides that no one shall be subjected to assault under any guise. The entire chapter 30 is dedicated to criminalising acts of indecent assault, abduction of females for sexual purposes, rape and attempted rape. The code also has provisions that punish child defilement, abandonment and battery. Unfortunately, Section 6 of the Criminal Code creates confusion as to whether marital rape is permitted in Nigeria. The section criminalises all forms of forced sexual intercourse except that which occurs between married couples.[150] The VAPP Act/Law in Section 1 criminalises all acts of forced intercourse but went short of expressly mentioning marital rape. This state of confusion must be clarified in subsequent amendment of the VAPP Act/Law to ensure that persons do not hide under the cover of marriage to defend acts of rape as the law is fuzzy on that area.

The Penal code is quite conservative in protecting women and girls from violence. Apart from the provisions which criminalise rape, trafficking and procurement for sex of women and girls in sections 282, 276 and 281 respectively, the Penal Code is largely silent on the protection of women from violence. Indeed and quite surprisingly, Section 55 of the code permits chastisement of a wife by her husband, even if she is an adult. This *imprimatur* to spousal violence against women is quite unfortunate and against the spirit of international human rights law.

Towards amending Defective Provisions within the Act

As noted in the introduction, The Violence against Persons Prohibition Act/ Law actually takes a broad perspective in defining what constitutes acts of violence. The Law prohibits all forms of sexual assault, intimidation,

---

[150] It defines unlawful carnal knowledge as a carnal connection which takes place otherwise than between husband and wife.

harassment and exploitation of any gender. It also aims to prevent all forms of negative cultural practices that have the capacity to violate the person or their property. In addition, the Act makes a novel provision of prohibiting and punishing economic abuse, verbal violence and isolation of a vulnerable person from family and friends. Female genital mutilation (FGM) is completely prohibited under Section 6 of the Act and a fine of N200, 000 or a four-year imprisonment or both were prescribed for such an act. Aiding and abetting this action attracts half the fine, a term of imprisonment or both. This paper notes that the punishment prescribed for FGM is too lenient and cannot discourage such violation which is deemed as a cultural rite in certain communities. Therefore, it proposes a fine of N500,000, or 10 years imprisonment or both for anyone who conducts such a grievous act of violence on a woman. In addition, all those who aided the act or encouraged it should be fined N300,000 or a five year imprisonment or both, to serve as a deterrent to others. Traditional rulers of such communities who deliberately allow such practice should lose their certificate of recognition or be suspended by the state government. It is proposed that the same punishment should be extended to other harmful traditional practices which impose untold violence on women and the girl child.

This paper recognises the fact that penal measures and custodial sentences in themselves are not sufficient to deter violators and prevent violence against women. Thus, the current state of the Act, which imposes only criminal sanctions, may not achieve the desired effect. Therefore, it is proposed that future amendments to the VAPP Act/Law should consider adopting the style of the Maputo Protocol by supplementing criminal sanction with public education on the dangers of violence against women. Non-custodial sentencing should also be adopted in appropriate cases. However, further amendments should clearly prohibit domestic settlement of violence against women as this has in many cases perpetuated acts of violence and led to the loss of lives.[151]

On rape, the VAPP Act/Law makes very elaborate provisions on when the offence is complete. It also extends the punishment from 14 years imposed

---

[151] If an act of violence should be settled outside the court system, then it should be by a proper mediation panel supervised by service providers and commitments to end violence must be binding and properly documented.

by the Criminal Code to life imprisonment. This is commendable and could go far to stem the tide of rape in the country. The Act also broadens the definition of rape to other forms of penetration beyond the vagina. Thus, anal penetration, even with the fingers, tongue or with any part of the body would be deemed to be rape. Hence, rape is no longer limited to vaginal penetration. However, the Act is silent on corroboration of rape allegation which has truncated most rape cases in Nigerian courts. Also, the requirement of having the victim personally give evidence in court reinforces the culture of silence as most victims would not want to expose themselves to re-telling lurid and painful experiences in the open court. Therefore, amendments to the VAPP Act/Law should consider accepting testimonies of the victim without audience in the courtroom. Moreover, the testimony of the victim and other surrounding evidence should be stated as sufficient corroborative evidence in all actions to prosecute rape. The Act should also criminalise any acts or attempted acts of intimidating or persuading the rape victim to drop their complaints or desist from pursuing justice in court.

Furthermore, the Act must clearly criminalise marital rape and settle this contentious issue in the Nigerian jurisprudence. The English Legal System, from where we copied the marital exemption, has since dispensed with that aberration. In most civilised crimes, marriage does not afford a cover for forced sexual intercourse. Therefore, an amended VAPP Law/Act should clearly prohibit all acts of forced sexual intercourse, including those occurring within the pendency of a valid marriage.

An amended VAPP Act/Law should create a special unit of the Police charged with the responsibility of responding to and protecting victims of violence. This is the best way to fully operationalise the provisions of Section 28 (1) of the VAPP Act which provides that a complainant may apply to the court to seek a protective order following an act or threat of violence. Granting this order is not an issue, but the challenge lies in the enforcement, as that would depend on the willingness of the Police to enforce the order of court. Therefore, a police unit in the guise of the special protection unit (which protects VIP's in Nigeria), should be established by the Act with a single mandate of enforcing such orders and generally implementing the provisions of the law. This would go a long way to ensure that Nigerians enjoy the protection of law as provided in the Act.

The Act also failed to make provisions to criminalise the re-victimisation of women and girls. There are reports that most victims of violence, particularly of the sexual type, are subjected to painful ordeals at the police stations and hospitals. Most police officers and health workers intimidate the victims by casting aspersions on their stories, harassing them and subjecting them to further disgrace. Amendments to the VAPP Act/Law, therefore, should prohibit all forms of victimisation or ridiculing of the complaint in any circumstance. Finally, a provision should be included in the law to reprimand parents or guardians whose acts of irresponsibility provided the opportunity for the girl-child to be violated. This would further ensure that minors are granted more protection within the family circle.

Conclusion

The Violence Against Persons Prohibition Act (2015) and the Enugu State VAPP Law (2019) have the potential to end the incidences of VAWG in Nigeria. However, the identified gaps must be covered in further amendments. Moreover, there is an urgent need to prioritise the implementation of these provisions by educating the public on the protections offered by these laws. Despite the flaws, the current state of the law is sufficient to protect women and girls if the police understand and apply the law dispassionately. Other stakeholders, particularly the judges, have to be educated on the roles of the court in protecting women and girls from violence. Courts should adopt a human rights-centred approach to interpreting the provisions of the Act/Law to ensure that the protection offered by the statute does not fall in the face of rigorous technicalities. It is time for Nigerian women and girls to feel the impact of the protection offered by this important piece of legislation. The collaboration of the legislature, police, prosecutors, the court and the public is therefore required to make this fully eradicate the incidence of violence against women and girls in Nigeria.

AN OVERVIEW OF THE ESSENTIAL ELEMENTS OF PHYSICAL AND SEXUAL VIOLENCE

Uju Peace Okeke

Abstract

Globally, violence in all its forms is abhorred and punished as crime. It defies gender, age, marital, economic, financial and other statuses. While everyone could suffer violence to a certain degree, some people are more susceptible due to a range of factors, necessitating greater protection. There are treaties at the international and regional levels offering general and specific protection from violence. Activists use these to make a case for the enactment of local legislation. Though Nigeria had laws penalising a few aspects of violence, it recently enacted a comprehensive Act protecting Nigerians from violence. In view of the presidential system of government, States are expected to localise this Act, and few have done so. Employing doctrinal methodology, using primary and secondary data sources, this work considers violence against persons in Nigeria. Relying on Violence Against Persons Prohibition Act and Violence Against Persons Prohibition Law of Enugu State, it discusses the meaning, forms, and elements of physical and sexual violence with their human rights dimension. It highlights features that make them consonant with today's reality. Applauding the holistic protection guaranteed in these laws, it concludes that in the absence of implementation fueled by purposeful awareness, the desire for a violence-free Nigeria will remain illusory.

1. Introduction

Human beings interact at different levels, publicly and privately, and sometimes in these relationships, violence occurs. It happens in the workplace, schools, and even in close relationships like families, involving men, women, young, old, single, married, rich and the poor. However, due to societal imbalances, some are more susceptible to violence; in this group, are women, girls, the aged, and disabled. Violence has become a global public health, human rights and development issue, attracting worldwide attention. Every day, we are inundated with news of different forms of interpersonal and collective violence by state and non-state actors.[152] The World Health Organization (WHO) reported that 3800 people die from violence every day. This translates to 1.4 million deaths, yearly. To worsen the situation, for every death from violence, many more suffer a range of injuries and other problems.[153] The world rose up against all forms of violence, paying special attention to the most vulnerable, through treaties and other international and regional human rights instruments, General Comments, General Recommendations and Special Resolutions. While some treaties directly protect against violence, almost all provide indirect protection. Directly, the International Covenant on Civil and Political Rights (ICCPR)[154] and the Convention on the Rights of the Child (CRC)[155] provided for it. The International Convention on the Elimination of All Forms of Discrimination against Women (CEDAW),[156] without mentioning violence, protects women from all its forms in different areas of its manifestations. At the regional level, the Protocol to the African Charter on Rights of women in Africa (African Women's Protocol),[157] ubiquitously protects African women from every imaginable form of violence.

* Department of Public Law, Faculty of Law, University of Nigeria, Nsukka, Enugu Campus (UNEC).

152 A 'Nigeria: Over 2,700 killed in 3 months of violence' https://www.aa.com.tr/en/africa/nigeria-over-2-700-killed-in-3-months-of-violence/1920052<ccessed 10 September 2020>.

153 WHO, '10 Facts About Violence Prevention' <https://www.who.int/features/factfiles/violence/en/> accessed 10 September 2020

154 Adopted and opened for signature, ratification and accession by General Assembly resolution 2200A (XXI) of 16 December 1966, entry into force 23 March 1976, ar 20.

155 Adopted and opened for signature, ratification and accession by General Assembly resolution 44/25 of 20 November 1989, entry into force 2 September 1990, ar 19.

156 Adopted and opened for signature, ratification and accession by General Assembly resolution 34/180 of 18 December 1979, entry into force 3 September 1981.

157 Adopted by the 2nd Ordinary Session of the African Union General Assembly in 2003 in Maputo CAB/LEG/66.6 (2003) entered into force 25 November, 2005, ars 3,4,5,11,23,.

International and regional treaties provide a standard for national legislation, thus, Nigeria, having ratified these treaties, has laws addressing violence. Nigeria operates a federal system of government wherein the National Assembly makes laws with regards to items in the Exclusive Legislative List but shares powers with States on items in the Concurrent Legislative List, with the Constitution sometimes setting out the scope for each tier. Therefore, there exist laws at the federal and state levels, addressing different forms of violence. At the federal level are the Criminal Code for the south,[158] and the Penal Code for the north.[159] The Child's Right Act (CRA) is a federal legislation dealing with children's concerns, one of which is violence.[160] Most states have localised the CRA. Recently, the National Assembly enacted the Violence against Persons Prohibition Act (VAPPA),[161] which holistically protects all persons from different aspects of violence in private or public life, providing meaningful remedies for victims while adequately punishing perpetrators to deter others. A few states have localised it in the form of Violence against Persons Prohibition Law (VAPPL)[162] and Domestic Violence Law (DVL).[163] The VAPPA/VAPPL are majorly concerned with secondary prevention, which are approaches that focus on the more immediate responses to violence, such as hospital care and other emergency services.[164] It is hoped that in the nearest future, primary and tertiary prevention and avoidance as well as long term rehabilitation and re-integration of victims will become points of emphasis.

2. Definition, Forms and Prevalence

Violence has been variously defined to include denial of rights, misuse of power, among others. WHO, the principal international health authority,

---

158 Criminal Code Act Chapter 77 Laws of the Federation of Nigeria 1990 ss 65(e), 195, 354, 401,.

159 Penal Code Law, 1959, Cap 89, Laws of Northern Nigeria, 1963 s.105.

160 The Nigerian Child's Rights Act 2003

161 Violence against Persons (Prohibition) Act, (VAPPA) 2015.

162 Violence against Persons (Prohibition) Law Oyo State, 2016; Violence against Persons (Prohibition) Law Anambra State, 2018; Violence against Persons (Prohibition) Law Kaduna State, 2018; Violence against Persons (Prohibition) Law No. 2 Enugu State, 2019; Violence against Persons (Prohibition) Law Bauchi State, 2020; Violence against Persons (Prohibition) Law Abia State, 2020; Violence against Persons (Prohibition) Law Kwara State, 2020;

163 Protection against Domestic Violence law of Lagos State No.15 2007

164 LL Dahlberg and EG. Krug 'Violence a global public health problem' (2006) *(11) (2) Ciência & Saúde Coletiva* 1413-8123.

defines it as 'the intentional use of physical force or power, threatened or actual, against oneself, another person, or against a group or community that either results in or has a high likelihood of resulting in injury, death, psychological harm, mal-development or deprivation.'[165] The VAPPA and VAPPL of Enugu state define it as "any act or attempted act, which causes or may cause any person physical, sexual, psychological, verbal, emotional or economic harm, whether this occurs in private or public life, in peace time and in conflict situations."[166] It is thus, an individual as much as collective affair and VAPPA/VAPPL, taking it beyond peace time, took into consideration our peculiarities such as community clashes, during which violence is visited on Nigerians.

2.1 Forms of Violence

The VAPPA/VAPPL Enugu identified six broad forms of violence: Physical, Sexual, Domestic, Economic, Harmful Traditional Practices and Emotional/Psychological/Verbal. Some acts of violence fall into more than one form.

2.1.1 Physical violence

This is an act of physical aggression towards another person, whether extreme or insignificant. It includes physical abuse, wrongful arrest and detention, assault, use of force without lawful authority, unlawful entry into properties, demolitions without due process, forced ejection from home, harassment, stalking, intimidation, spousal battery, substance attack. The VAPPA/VAPPL, in recognising spousal battery as violence, make it easier for law enforcement officers to prosecute perpetrators, unlike before, when they considered it a family affair, undeserving of investigation and prosecution.

2.1.2 Sexual violence

This is considered one of the most traumatic and common forms of violence, affecting physical and mental health, with reproductive right implication. It occurs in times of peace and armed conflict, perpetrated by state and non-state actors. It is defined as any or attempt of an act that violates sexual

---

[165] World Health Organization. 'Global consultation on violence and health. Violence: a public health priority' Geneva: WHO; 1996 (document WHO/EHA/SPI. POA.2).

[166] VAPPA (n 10) s 46; VAPPL Enugu State (n 11) s.2.

integrity of another,[167] that is, obtaining sexual act by force or coercion. It includes sexual assault of unlawful touching, striking, sexual exploitation of forced prostitution, sexual harassment, sexual intimidation for promotion, employment, patronage, etc. It is worthy of note that the VAPPA and VAPPLs retained life imprisonment as punishment for rape but re-defined it in a novel manner that brings it in consonance with laws in other jurisdictions. Unlike the Criminal Code and Penal Code that saw rape as penile penetration of vagina, the VAPPA/VAPPL see it as committed by anyone (male or female) through the penetration of vagina, anus or mouth with penis or any body part. These laws penalise maximally, acts which, hitherto, were considered at best assault, attracting lenient punishment. The VAPPA further provides for appropriate compensation[168] for victims of rape which has the effect of breaking the culture of silence around it.

2.1.3 Psychological/Emotional/Verbal violence

This is a pattern of degrading or humiliating conduct towards a person. It is a manifestation of power imbalance in a relationship, wherein the perpetrator uses it to maintain control over the victim. Such conducts include insults, ridicule, repeated exhibition of obsessive possessiveness invading liberty, forced isolation from family, entry into the complainant's residence without consent. The VAPPA/VAPPL seem to strongly suggest that emotional violence is considered as serious as physical violence.

2.1.4 Domestic violence

It is an act perpetrated on any person in a domestic relationship causing harm to the safety, health, or well-being of any person. Domestic relationship is one between a person and a perpetrator of violence where they are or were married to each other, live or lived together in a marriage-like relationship, are the parents of a child, are family members, are or were engaged, in actual or perceived intimate relationship and/or share or recently shared same residence.[169] Intimate partner violence is rife in domestic relationships but others equally suffer violence, including children, domestic servants and other family members. In fact, children who only witness violence are considered

---

[167] VAPPL Enugu State (n11) s.2

[168] VAPPA (n10) s 1(3)

[169] VAPPL Enugu State (n11) s.3

victims too. In *NPF & Ors v Omotosho & Ors*,[170] the unlawful killing of a man by a police officer, before his wife and children, was held to violate their right to dignity. Clearly, all the identified forms of violence may take place in a domestic relationship. The VAPPA/VAPPL prohibit different forms of violence in many Nigerian settings which were previously considered normal correctional measures in families.

2.1.5 Economic violence

This is denial of inheritance and other economic resources that one is entitled to. It comprises abandonment of dependants without sustenance; denial of inheritance; deprivation of financial resources, including household necessities; damage to property; starvation; and denial of basic education. Women bear the greater brunt of economic violence due to past neglect and cultural practices treating them as *res*, stripping them of the right to possess property. It is said that poverty wears the face of a woman as 70% of citizens living below the poverty line are women.[171]

2.1.6 Harmful traditional practices

This embraces all traditional behaviours and practices affecting fundamental rights of any person. The pieces of legislation proscribe different forms of violence perpetrated in the guise of culture like widowhood practices, forced marriages, female genital cutting (FGC), among others. FGC is prevalent as 68 per cent of Nigerian females have undergone it.[172] It is rooted in religion, culture[173] and poverty as circumcisers need it as a source of income and families need it to ensure their daughters' marriage which is also a source of income as her husband becomes financially available. In prohibiting this sort of violence, the VAPPA/VAPPL conforms to section 21 of the Constitution[174] which calls for the protection, preservation and promotion of positive and dignity- enhancing cultures. It is also in agreement with court decisions in

---

170 (2018) LPELR-45778(CA)

171 National Gender Policy .

172 'Giving up Harmful Practices, Not Culture' <http://www.advocatesforyouth.org/Publications/iag/harmprac.htm> accessed 10 September 2020.

173 Ibid.

174 Constitution of the Federal Republic of Nigeria (Promulgation) Act, (as amended)1999, Cap C23, Vol. 3, Laws of the Federation of Nigeria, 2004

Mojekwu v Mojekwu,[175] where *oliekpe* custom that disinherits women in the absence of surviving sons in intestacy was pronounced discriminatory and repugnant to natural justice, equity and good conscience. Further, it justifies the Court of Appeal decision in *Theresa Onwo v Nwafor Oko & 12 Ors*,[176] where a widow was compelled to shave her hair and perform other culturally accepted widowhood rites against her wish and religious belief. The court held that the cultural observation breached her right to personal dignity, entitling her to remedies.

2.2 Prevalence

Violence against women is rife. They are usually targets of sexual violence due to existing inequality between men and women. Worldwide, 40 to 47 per cent of sexual assaults are perpetrated on girls aged 15 or younger, and in Nigeria, 81 per cent of young girls in hawking business undergo sexual violence.[177] Other researches reveal that domestic violence is also very pervasive, particularly against women who are made to endure emotional violence as a mark of submission.[178] Other manifestations of the domestic violence include maltreatment of domestic staff,[179] intimate partner abuse[180] even during pregnancy[181] and defilement of girls by known perpetrators.[182]

---

175 (1997) 7 NWLR Pt 512;283

176 (1996) 6 NWLR (PT 456) 584

177 'Prevalence and Nature of Violence among Young Female Hawkers in Motor-parks in South-Western Nigeria' <http://www.emeraldinsight.com/Insight/ViewContentServlet?Filename=Published/EmeraldFullTextArticle/Articles/1421020503.html> accessed 10 September 2020; SL Delano 'Sexual Abuse and Violence in sub-Saharan Africa' (2007) *Advocates for Youths* <http://www.advocatesforyouth.org/publications/factsheet/fssxabus.htm>accessed 10 September 2020.

178 ON Aihie 'Prevalence of domestic violence in Nigeria: implications for counseling' 2(1) Edo Journal of Counseling 2010

179 'Residents storm court as magistrate remands Enugu couple over abuse of 10-year-old maid' The Guardian <https://guardian.ng/news/residents-storm-court-as-magistrate-remands-enugu-couple-over-abuse-of-10-year-old-maid/> accessed 10 September 2020

180 C Ezeudu, and Others, 'Prevalence and correlates of Intimate Partner Violence among Women attending Child Health Services, Enugu State, Nigeria' (2015) (82) (3) *Annals of Global Health* 416.

181 RC Onoh and Others, 'Prevalence, Pattern and Consequences of Intimate Partner Violence During Pregnancy at Abakaliki Southeast Nigeria' (2013) (3) (4) *Ann Med Health Sci Res* 484

182 RS Ohayi and Others, 'Prevalence and Pattern of Rape among Girls and Women attending Enugu State University Teaching Hospital, Southeast Nigeria' (2015) (130) (1) *International Journal of Gynaecology and Obstetrics* 13

The nation witnessed an increase in domestic violence during the Covid-19 lockdown.[183] The widespread violence against women and children, especially in domestic relationships, may not be far from the patriarchal nature of the Nigerian society. It follows that preventing sexual and physical violence against women will require a deliberate collective initiative by men,[184] through cultural re-orientation, legislation, and economic empowerment of women.

3. Elements of Physical and Sexual Violence

Sexual and physical violence are somewhat interlinked as sexual violence may involve physical violence while physical violence could degenerate to sexual violence. Generally, in our criminal law jurisprudence, there are two elements of an offence which must exist before conviction. They are *mens rea* and *actus reus*, Latin words which mean guilty mind and guilty act respectively. They two must be proved except in strict liability cases where *mens rea* flows into *actus reus*.[185]

Various offences of a sexual nature are criminalised by the Criminal Code[186] and the Penal Code.[187] Of all these offences, rape seems to be the most serious, attracting the most severe penalty of life imprisonment. The apex court defined it in the case of *Posu v State*[188] as 'an unlawful carnal knowledge of a woman by a man who is not her husband, to have sexual intercourse forcibly without her consent.' It is still rape if the consent is obtained by force or by means of threat or intimidation of any kind or by fear of harm, or by means of false and fraudulent representation as to the nature of the act or in the case of a married woman by impersonating her husband.

Section 1 of VAPPA and section 3 of VAPPL, Enugu have almost similar provisions on rape. The VAPPA provides -

---

183 WACOL Condemns Increased cases of Violence against Women, Girls' Business Day June 7 2020 https://businessday.ng/news/article/wacol-condemns-increased-cases-of-violence-against-women-girls/ accessed 10 September 2020

184 EG Krug and Others, 'World report on violence and health' (eds) 169 (1-360) WHO Geneva 2002

185 *Abeke v State (2007) LPELR-31(SC)* Per Niki Tobi J.S.C.

186 Criminal Code (n 7) S.357

187 Penal Code (n 8) S.282

188 (2011) 2 NWLR (Pt. 1234) P. 392 @ 414 -416

(1) A person commits the offence of rape if (a) he intentionally penetrates the vagina, anus or mouth of another person with any other part of his or her body or anything else; (b) the other person does not consent to the penetration; or (c) the consent is obtained by force or means of threat or intimidation of any kind or by fear of harm or by means of fraud and fraudulent representation as to the nature of the act or the use of any substance or addictive capable of taking away the will of such a person or in the case of a married person by impersonating his or her spouse.

There is a slight variation in (1)(a), VAPPL Enugu provides that rape can be said to have occurred if the perpetrator '(a) intentionally penetrates the vagina, anus or mouth of another person **no matter how slight with his sex organ** or any other part of his or her body or anything else.' Being a newer legislation that came into force, four years after the VAPPA, it seems to have the intention of elucidating that rape will be committed at the least penetration.

While the Criminal/Penal Codes, and the VAPPA/VAPPL, define rape differently to a certain extent, they share similar features. Flowing from the above the features are:

a) The perpetrator must have *mens rea*

Mens rea is concerned with the intention to commit an act, in this case, rape. It means that the act complained of is not accidental as the perpetrator intended to rape the complainant without her/his consent. Intention does not excuse reckless acts, thus in *Posu v State*,[189] the Supreme Court held that intention is imputed where the perpetrator acted recklessly, not caring whether the victim consented or not. This is also clear in the WHO's definition of violence in associating intention with the act, irrespective of the outcome.[190] For other forms of sexual and physical violence, the act complained of could be of commission or omission. An example is spousal battery which is the unlawful use of force upon a person, thus commission, while abandonment is deliberately leaving perpetrator's dependants destitute, and without any means of subsistence. It follows that abandonment would be committed where

---

189 Ibid.

190 World Health Organization (n 14).

the perpetrator does not deliberately take the action of removing necessaries from the dependants but through inaction, fails to provide them with means of subsistence.

b) Penetration

Under the Criminal/Penal Codes, the penetration must be penile and of vagina, though the rupture of the hymen is unnecessary to establish rape – *Idi v State.*[191] In fact, the Supreme Court said that penetration is the most important ingredient of the offence of rape as it is complete upon proof of penetration – *Posu v State.*[192] Again, the penetration must be penile and of the vagina unlike the present VAPPA/VAPPL, where the penetration could be of vagina, anus or mouth and by penile, any other body part or object. This has broadened the otherwise narrow definition of the Criminal/ Penal Codes and court interpretations of them which in effect is allowing some rapists escape the law. This is necessary as in practice, non-penile penetration with other harmful objects that are more demeaning on which punishment at best, will only amount to a lesser offence of indecent assault with lesser penalty. This puts Nigeria at par with other African jurisdictions like South Africa.[193]

c) The victim did not consent or consented under duress and intimidation

A legitimate act must be consented to which evidences that the act is wanted. Violence, whether physical or sexual, is usually unwanted, happening without the consent of the victim. The Criminal/Penal Code and the VAPPA/VAPPL are in agreement that rape must be without consent of the victim. This suggests that consent nullifies the offence of rape – *Posu v State.*[194] However, the consent must be real and not one obtained fraudulently or by intimidation or misrepresentation. In the absence of consent, an act is unwanted whether or not force was applied.[195] Sometimes, the law determines what is wanted at

---

[191] *(2016) LPELR-41555(CA)*

[192] *Posu v State* (n 37).

[193] S v Masiya 2006(2) SACR 357.

[194] *Posu v State* (n 37).

[195] UN Women, 'Definition of Sexual Assault and other Elements' https://www.endvawnow.org/en/articles/453-definition-of-sexual-assault-and-other-elements.html

a particular stage. For instance, a minor is incapable of consenting to sex, thus an adult who gets sexually involved with a minor cannot escape punishment by claiming that the minor wanted it.

d) The perpetrator and the victim are not married to themselves

The Criminal/Penal Code and the VAPPA/VAPPL definition exclude a husband from rape, meaning that marital rape is not an offence in Nigeria. It follows that for an act to be considered rape, it must involve non-marriage partners. While there have been complaints of marital rape, Nigerian laws are yet to boldly legislate against it as in other jurisdictions.

e) Gender of perpetrator

There is a sharp distinction on who can commit the act of rape from the angle of the Criminal/Penal Code and the VAPPA/VAPPL. Before the coming into force of the latter laws, our courts, in line with the provisions of Criminal and Penal Codes, interpreted that a man cannot be raped in Nigeria. The VAPPA/VAPPL has changed this interpretation, meaning that a man as well as a woman could experience rape. It equally re-defined the act of rape to include other sexual acts like anal and oral sex, which were hitherto not recognised and thus unpunished.

VAPPA and VAPPL strongly indicate other features of violence, non-essential and harmful.[196]

f) The act must be Non-essential

Another feature of physical and sexual violence is that the act complained of is usually unnecessary to further the aim of a lawful action. For instance if a husband uses spousal battery to settle spousal conflict, the battery is needless as the conflict could be resolved without the battery.[197] This could be the reason for the comprehensive provision in the VAPPA/VAPPL that 'victim' includes the sufferer of the violence, the immediate family, dependants and anyone who suffers harm in assisting the direct victim. However, Section 35 of the Constitution excuses some seemingly non-

---

196 S Hamby 'On Defining Violence and why it Matters' 2017 (7) (2) *Psychology of Violence* 167.

197 Ibid.

essential acts which ordinarily would constitute violence under the VAPPA/VAPPL, if the procedure is permitted by law. These are acts that infringe on personal liberty but are carried on in execution of courts' sentence, for the welfare and education of a child, for prevention of unlawful entry into Nigeria and for the treatment of vagrant, insane and sufferer of infectious disease or addiction.

g) The act must be Harmful

The violent act must be harmful.[198] From the provisions of the VAPPA/VAPPL, harm has a broad definition and need not be only physical, like when death occurs. Psychological damage that erodes autonomy, impacting on dignity and privacy, suffices. This is understandable as some harms are hidden, going by the effects of violence which include poor bodily image, low self-esteem, depression, suicide bout, poor health results, loss of job or productivity and breaching of human rights. The element of harm might have informed the VAPPA in section 1(3) providing for the award of compensation which personally benefits the victim even as perpetrator is punished for the act.

4. Human Rights Dimension

One of the effects of violence is that it violates constitutionally guaranteed human rights. Some of the rights violated are rights to life, dignity and freedom from discrimination.

4.1 Right to life

Acts of violence, particularly physical, sexual and harmful traditional practices, happening in a domestic relationship or elsewhere could lead to death, breaching right to life. Right to life has been described as the fulcrum of the other rights, a fundamental right in the absence of which other rights make no sense.[199] This is the reason Murder is criminalised by sections 306 and 308 of the Criminal Code. Section 33(1) of the Constitution provides that '*every person has a right to life, and no one shall be deprived intentionally*

---

198 Ibid.

199 RJ Cook and BM Dickens and MF Fathalla, *Reproductive Health and Human Rights: Integrating Medicine, Ethics and Law* (Oxford: Clarendon Press 2003)11.

of his life, save in execution of the sentence of a court ...' The constitutional provision seems to be in total agreement with the importance of this right as it implies that any death not flowing from execution of court sentence is a violation of the right to life.[200] The death of Nigerians through violence, whether by force, starvation, sexual abuse, aggression, cultural practices, among others, breaches this right.

4.2 Right to Dignity of human person

Dignity, the foundation of other human rights inheres in every human being. It is the right to be treated like a human being and section 34(1) (a) of the Nigerian Constitution provides that '*every individual is entitled to respect for the dignity of his person, and accordingly no person shall be subjected to torture or inhuman or degrading treatment...*' Violence is nothing but blatant torture. The Court of Appeal held in *Uzoukwu & 5 Ors v Ezeonu II & 8 Ors (1991) 6 NWLR (Pt. 200) 708*, that torture include '...brutalization of the human body or a mental torture in the sense of mental agony or mental worry. Degrading treatment has the element of lowering the societal status, character, value or position of a person...' Physical and verbal violence degrades. Rape of any sort is demeaning and violates sexual and health rights of victims while harmful traditional practices are torturous. WHO defines health as 'a state of complete physical, mental and social well-being and not merely the absence of disease or infirmity.'[201] Following this definition, rape destroys all aspects of well-being – physical because of the force involved; mental because of the trauma; and social because of the resultant stigma which is worse if the victim gets pregnant and gives birth to a rape-child.

---

200 UP Okeke 'A case for the Enforcement of Women's Rights as Human Rights in Nigeria' in K.O Irabor (ed): *New Thoughts in the Administration of Justice*, (Lagos: Elim Prints & Publications 2009), 164.

201 14 UNTS 185 The Constitution of WHO was adopted by the International Health Conference, New York 19-22 June, 1945; opened for signature on 22nd July 1946 by the representatives of 61 states (official records of the World Health Organisation, no.2 p.100); and entered into force on 7 April 1948. WHO in the preamble to its constitution of 1946 proclaimed that 'the enjoyment of the highest attainable standard of living is one of the fundamental rights of every human being without distinction of race, religion, political belief, economic or social condition'; C Ngwena& R Cook 'Rights Concerning Health' in Brand D &Heyns C (eds) Socio-economic Rights in South Africa (2005) 109.

4.3 Right to Freedom from Discrimination

Discrimination is a particular form of differentiation irrespective of intention.[202] Section 42(1) of the Constitution provides for right to non-discrimination on a plethora of grounds including sex, particular community, birth circumstances. Many people suffer violence due to sex, thus reports abound that more women than men suffer violence. A 2019 poll confirmed prevalent domestic violence particularly by men.[203] Male perpetrators, through violence, exhibit their supremacy over women, who they consider powerless in many ways. The societal biases also put women at a disadvantageous position therefore, more women than men go through harmful traditional practices like FGC and widowhood malpractices. Due to patriarchy, more women suffer economic violence as traditionally, women are only allowed family inheritance on rare occasions. Factors like son preference and child marriage make women economically dependent on men.[204]

5. Recommendations

Laws exhibit government's will in solving a problem. The VAPPA/VAPPLs evidence government's will and provides an enabling environment for the eradication of violence against persons in Nigeria. The enactment of VAPPA/ VAPPLs, though a giant step, is not a magic wand that will eradicate violence in the absence of awareness and implementation. Addressing violence will begin from the description of its magnitude and impact. Now that Nigeria has declared it unlawful, long lasting success will depend on comprehensive approach involving multi-sectoral partnerships of stakeholders who must engage the law and demand for structures that will ensure success. Some forms of violence are invisible, meaning that some perpetrators do not know their actions constitute violence, it behoves stakeholders to disseminate the VAPPA/VAPPL to all, empowering perpetrators with knowledge of acts to desist from as ignorance of law is no excuse, and victims with knowledge of acts to forbid. As prevention is significant and education is key, training and re-training of all, beginning with law enforcement officers, is necessary. These officers constitute a major implementing stakeholder bloc such that

[202] UP Okeke (n 49).

[203] NOI Polls 'Domestic Violence Polls' https://noi-polls.com/wp-content/uploads/2019/11/ Domestic-Violence-Press-Release-2019.pdf

[204] UP Okeke (n 49).

improving their professionalism will place them in a position to protect Nigerians against violence, especially the vulnerable groups.

6. Conclusion

Accumulation of small cruelties leads to societal decay that will affect everyone; little wonder violence has become a significant public health concern. Violence has short and long-term consequences, one of which is depletion of the states' resources in terms of legal cost of prosecuting perpetrators; health care cost of victims; their loss of earnings and by extension, taxes government would have earned from their productivity.[205] Seeing that violence is an evil wind that blows no one any good, it is time for all the stakeholders and lovers of a violence-free Nigeria (comprising of government, law enforcement agents, media, educational institutions, courts, religious cum traditional rulers, civil society groups, non-governmental organisations and individuals, human and women's rights activists) to stand against violence using the veritable tool – VAPPA/VAPPL.

[205] Dahlberg (n 13).

RAPE AND PROSECUTION CHALLENGES IN NIGERIA

By Daniel Ikechukwu Onyeonagu Esq.
(LL.B, BL, LL.M)

Lecturer in Faculty of Law, Department of International and Comparative Law, University of Nigeria, Nsukka

ABSTRACT

Despite decades of feminist activism, and avalanche of laws to tame the scourge of rape, the menace continues to escalate at appalling rates. This paper explores an understanding of rape and the challenges of prosecuting rape cases in Nigeria. The paper concludes with recommendations on ways and means of tackling this social menace in Nigeria.

1.0. INTRODUCTION

Rape may be defined as sexual penetration of a woman against her will. It has been argued that reforms have extended the definition to include any bodily orifice.[206] Rape, in legal parlance, means a forcible sexual intercourse with a woman without the woman giving her consent to it. In law, any person who has unlawful carnal knowledge of a woman or girl, without her consent, or if the consent is obtained by force or by means of threats or intimidation of any kind or by fear of harm or by means of false and fraudulent representation as to the nature of the act, is guilty of the offence of rape.[207]

2.0 Violence Against Persons (Prohibition) Act 2015 states that rape is committed when a person intentionally penetrates the vagina, anus or mouth of another person with any other part of his/her body or anything

---

206 The Encyclopedia America - International Edition, Vol. 23, Crolie Incorporated, (1988) P. 185

207 See Oludotun Ogunbayo V. The State (2007) LPELR-2323(SC), Sections 357 of the Criminal and penal Codes respectively.

else without consent, or with incorrectly obtained consent where such consent was obtained by force/threats/intimidation, false and fraudulent representation as to the nature of the act, use of substances capable of taking away the will of that person, or impersonating a married woman's husband in order to have sex with her.[208] The use of the word 'person' or 'his/her' in Section 1 of VAPP Act, 2015 expands the application of the offence of rape to include men or boys.

4.0. ELEMENTS OF THE OFFENCE OF RAPE

For an offence of rape to be committed, there must be present, the *actus reus*[209] (actual performance of the offence) and the *mens rea* (mental element/ intention to commit the offence). Section 24 of the Criminal Code provides that:

> *"Subject to the express provisions of the Code relating to negligent acts and omissions, a person is not criminally responsible for an act or omission, which occurs independently of the exercise of his will, or for an event which occurs by accident."*

It is a basic and fundamental requirement in most cases to prove that the accused committed the *actus reus* in a particular state of mind. In essence, it has to be proved that he intended his actions, or knew the resultant effect of his action. In order words, he intended what he did. In the case of rape, it is a basic requirement for conviction of an accused person, to prove that his action of having carnal knowledge of another, was intended. Section 24 of the Criminal Code is therefore a defense to an accused person if the alleged act of rape was committed independent of the exercise of his will.

5.0. INGREDIENTS OF RAPE

i. Penetration

There cannot be an offence of rape without proof of penetration.[210] In order to prove penetration, it is not necessary to prove that the hymen was ruptured

---

208 S. 1 of Violence Against Persons (Prohibition) Act, 2015

209 Williams, G., & Smith, A. T. H: Learning the law. (London: Sweet & Maxwell 2006) 18

210 R. v Kufi (1960) W.N.L.R. 1

or that there has been an emission of semen. The slightest penetration of the vagina is sufficient to prove the offence.[211] This, in essence, means that the offence of rape is complete upon penetration.[212]

ii. Consent

Absence of consent is paramount in order to establish a case of rape. The prosecution must prove that the accused person had carnal knowledge of the woman or girl without her consent.[213] In the case of *R v Kufi*, the court held that the fact that the woman or girl is a common prostitute and that she has consented to intercourse on other occasions with the accused person or even that she is his concubine is not an excuse to have carnal knowledge of her without her consent. That notwithstanding, while reaching a decision in the instant case, the above stated facts may weigh on the mind of the court and possibly constitute a reason not to believe the woman or girl's denial of consent.[214]

Consent must be given willingly. When it is gotten by force, intimidation, threat, fear of harm, or given because of exhaustion after persistent struggle and resistance it may not avail the accused person a successful defence. It is a general principle of law that fraud vitiates consent.[215] In the same vein, submission by a person of weak intellect or a person who is too young to understand the nature of the act done is not consent.

iii. Capacity

Capacity to commit the offence of rape is paramount in determining whether the offence has been committed or not.

a. A male person below 12 years of age

As provided in Section 30 of the Criminal Code, a male person under the age of 12 years is presumed to be incapable of having carnal

---

211 S. 6 of the Criminal Code

212 Ibid.

213 R. v Kufi, supra

214 Ibid.

215 R. v Flattery (1877) 2 Q. B. D. 410

knowledge. To this effect, such a male person cannot be guilty of the offence of rape or attempted rape although he may be convicted of indecent assault.[216] The presumption is one of law and this presumption cannot be rebutted by proving that the accused has reached the full state of puberty even though he is below the age of 12 years.

b. Spousal rape

Spousal rape is a situation where a man has sexual intercourse with his wife, to whom he is lawfully married, without her consent. That is, non-consensual sexual intercourse with a spouse, however obtained may not be a crime. However, there is a growing trend that marital exemption is unjust and has no place in a civilised society.[217] For centuries, husbands around the world were granted marital exemption to the crime of rape. It was not until the last half of the twentieth century that marital rape was even recognised as a legal problem. It raises a pertinent question whether marital rape is known to our laws.

1. Can a husband rape his wife? (Prior to passing into law of VAPP Law or Act)

Prior to passing into law of the Violence Against Persons (Prohibition) Act[218] which some states in Nigeria have adopted, the general view was that a husband cannot be guilty of rape upon his wife.[219] This privilege of a man not being capable of committing rape against his wife is limited by the following:

a. An order for dissolution of the marriage, or
b. An order for judicial separation.

When either of the above orders is still subsisting, the implied consent to intercourse given by the wife at marriage is thereby revoked and it will amount to rape for the husband to have sex without the wife's consent.[220] The

---

216 S. 176 of the Criminal Procedure Act

217 Fus, T. "Criminalizing Marital Rape: A Comparison of Judicial and Legislative Approach". Vanderbilt Journal of Transnational Law (01-March-06) available at http://www.accesssmylibrary.comlcom2/summary 0286- 17461960 ITM (accessed on 15 September, 2020)

218 2015

219 S. 6 of the Criminal Code

220 R v Clarke (1949) 33 Cr. App. R. 216

implied consent of a wife to intercourse is not revoked by the mere fact that she has presented a petition for divorce.[221] In a situation where a husband makes an undertaking "not to assault, molest or otherwise interfere with his wife…", such undertaking is equivalent to an injunction and has the effect of revoking the implied consent to intercourse.[222] Even though a husband may not be guilty of rape upon his wife, he may be guilty of assault or wounding if he uses force or violence to exercise his right to intercourse. As provided in Section 7 of the Criminal Code, where a person lacks the capacity to commit the offence of rape, such a person may still be charged with the offence of aiding, counselling or procuring the commission of the offence.[223]

Under the **Criminal Code**[224], rape can only be committed by a man upon a woman or girl, as a woman cannot be guilty of the offence upon a man. **Section 6 of the Criminal Code** provides:

> *"When the term "carnal knowledge" or the term "carnal connection" is used in defining an offence, it is implied that the offence, so far as regards that element of it, is complete upon penetration.*
>
> *"unlawful carnal knowledge" means carnal connection which takes place otherwise than between husband and wife."*

Section 357 of the Code states:

> *Any person who has unlawful carnal knowledge* ***of a woman or girl****, without her consent, or with her consent, if the consent is obtained by force or by means of threats or intimidation of any kind, or by fear of harm, or by means of false and fraudulent representation as to the*

---

221 R v Miller (1954) 2 Q. B. 282

222 R v Steele (1977) Crim. L.R. 290

223 R v Cogan and Leak [1975] Crim. L.R 584 See also R v Ram (1893) 17 Cox 609 – A husband raped his maid. His wife was, however, convicted alongside as a principal offender in the second degree.

224 S. 357 of the Criminal Code

> *nature of the act, or, in the case of a married woman, by impersonating her husband, is guilty of an offence which is called rape.*

From the above, it can be deduced that under the Criminal Code as provided in Sections 6 and 357:

a. Marital rape is not recognised.
b. Only a woman or girl can be raped

2. Can a husband rape his wife? (Post VAPP Act)

Under VAPP Act, either a man or a woman can commit the offence of rape. Section 1 of the Act provides that:

> *"a person commits rape, if he or she intentionally penetrates the vagina, anus or mouth of another person with any part of his or her body or anything else, and without the consent of the other person."*

By implication, it could be deduced that under the VAPP Act,

a. Marital rape could be recognised because there is no express limitation as to who the section should apply to.
b. Either a man or woman/girl can be raped.
c. Rape could be perpetration with a part of the body or even with an object.

VAPP Act did not define the offence of rape. The interpretation of Section 1 of the Act is yet to be tested in Nigerian Courts, but it is an opinion that "a person…if he or she" as used in Section 1 of the Act refer to both men and women/girls alike.

One of the very notable and commendable provisions of VAPP Act is its expansion of the meaning of rape and its prohibition thereof. While other existing laws limited their scope of rape to protect only females in relation to vaginal penetration without consent, the VAPP Act has taken a giant stride to expand the meaning and scope of rape. By virtue of the Act, rape is when a person intentionally penetrates the vagina, anus or mouth of another person with any other part of his or her body or anything else without consent, or where such consent is obtained by force or by means of threat or intimidation of any kind or by fear of harm or by means of false and fraudulent representation as to the nature of the act or the use of any substance or additive capable of taking away the will of such person or in the case of a married person by impersonating his or her spouse. By this provision, both males and females are protected against rape. The issue of rape being gender biased has been a jurisprudential issue in Nigeria for a while because our law, as it then was, did not recognise situations wherein a man would or could be raped.

The Act, also, in its progressive nature, took cognisance of the fact that sex now goes beyond the primary sex organs and thus, extended the scope of rape to include anus and mouth. This is because it was difficult in times past, to bring an issue of forceful anal or oral sex under the umbrella of rape simply because such occasion was not envisaged or accommodated by our laws.

6.0. CHALLENGES OF PROSECUTION OF RAPE CASES IN NIGERIA

The Nigerian legal system is not left out in the challenges facing the prosecution of rape offences in Nigeria. Such challenges include:

a. Compounding Felony

There are instances where in rape cases the prosecution is faced with the challenge of compounding felony by the complainant or victim. The decision by a victim of a **crime** to not prosecute the **crime** (by refusing to co-operate with the police or prosecuting attorney) or to hamper the prosecution, in exchange for money payment or other recompense.[225]

In many instances, rape cases are settled even at the back of the prosecutors by family members and friends of the parties involved, leaving the prosecutor helpless in court as often times, such complainants would stop attending proceedings in court. This recurrent decimal frustrates the efforts of prosecutors in effectively prosecuting rape cases.

---

225 Section 127 of the Criminal Code; https://www.law.cornell.edu/wex/compounding_a_felony (assessed 16 September, 2020)

b. Many Prosecutors are Overwhelmed with Modern Technology

Many prosecutors in rape cases face an ever-increasing array of challenges and responsibilities, including storing, and using growing bodies of evidence generated through modern technology. Some of these issues have emerged recently, while others represent ongoing challenges to prosecutors that have been complicated by recent technology or emerging trends. Prosecutors are expected to be diligent at work while balancing aspects of budgets and resources, working with increasingly larger volumes of digital and electronic evidence that have developed from technological advancements (such as social media platforms) and being held accountable for their actions and differing litigation strategies. State and local prosecutors around the country continue to contend with very high caseloads and comparatively meagre salaries. Advances in forensic science have brought new capabilities that can be critical to a case. With the advent of such technology as social media and body-worn cameras, prosecutors must contend with large volumes of digital information and must determine the admissibility of evidence based on not just its probative value, but also whether a proper chain of custody was established and followed. These realities can make both the retention and the ongoing professional development of prosecution a challenge.

c. Training

Proper and regular training of prosecutors is essential, but it can be difficult for more experienced prosecutors to make time for training on top of their regular workloads and other professional demands. For example, there is currently a lack of training on how to effectively use technology at trials. This issue is compounded by the costs associated with bringing in outside expertise to help prepare and present complex digital evidence. Some more experienced prosecutors may also be reluctant to adapt to new technologies. Furthermore, the promises of new technologies (e.g., using virtual tools to allow testimony from experts) are not always realised or possible. Prosecutors and others involved in the criminal justice system should be trained about the limitations of certain types of evidence.

d. Delay in Duplication of Case Files and Receiving DPP's Advice

Delay in the dispensation of justice is one of the major challenges facing prosecutors in carrying out their duties. This has been a subject of several discussions and interventions in recent times. Criminal trials are often delayed, especially in cases where persons standing trial have the means to engage the services of legal practitioners who could exploit the gaps in law to the advantage of their clients especially in delaying proceedings. Sometimes, matters are referred to the office of the Director of Public Prosecution for advice. In most cases, it takes many months before the said advice would be available for the prosecutor. This delay has often led to such unduly delayed matter being struck out for want of diligent prosecution.

Part of the duties of an investigating police officer is to have case files duplicated and transmitted to the office of the Director of Public Prosecutions for legal advice, especially where serious offences and technical offences are involved. As straight forward as this process is, it has constituted a major bottleneck in the Nigerian criminal justice system. Some criminal matters have been known to be bogged down at this stage of the criminal administration of justice for up to two years and more. The Nigeria Police investigators place the blame for the non-duplication and the delayed duplication of investigation case files on the non- availability of duplicating equipment and services at police stations. Most times, police investigators have had to resort to commercial duplicating service providers, with the attendant risks of mutilation, loss and the premature exposure of investigation reports in the public media, sometimes leading to prejudicial consequences. The funds for duplications at commercial centres have had to be sourced from the police investigators' personal purses, the complainants, the victims or from the accused persons with the threat that otherwise, such a case would remain at a standstill.[226]

e. Unnecessary Adjournments at the Instance of the Defence To Frustrate the Case

It is the practice by some mischievous legal practitioners to seek for unending adjournments in cases in court, including rape cases, in a bid to frustrate the case. In some instances, the complainant or victim as well as other prospective witnesses could get discouraged from attending further proceedings. This leaves the prosecutor helpless in the course of prosecuting the case. Many cases are struck out for want of diligent prosecution as a result of continuous

226 https://tribuneonlineng.com/delay-major-challenge-of-nigerian-criminal-justice-system-%E2%80%95-oyo-cj/ (accessed 16 September, 2020)

absence of the necessary witnesses. In some instances, this might create a loophole in the evidence before the court which (inures) in favour of the accused person.

7.0. CONCLUSION

In this paper, rape was defined and the challenges of prosecution of rape cases highlighted. The work also looked at the criminal justice system and how it encourages the crime of rape in Nigeria. It is, therefore, recommended that there is a need for the review of the law on rape in Nigeria to expand the definition and make it an all-encompassing offence for both sexes. It is also recommended that the process of the trial of rape offences should be reviewed. The State should make provisions for the victims of rape and provide counsellors for them where necessary. Similarly, the State should set up special courts to try offences of rape and where possible, in camera, to protect the virtues or dignity of the victim. Prosecution for the offence of rape should be wholly state sponsored and the victim should remain what she is in law which is, a witness. Victims/survivors of sexual violence should be given all the help they need and government must be ready to investigate and prosecute sexual offences. Courts must not unnecessarily delay the prosecution of these cases by unending adjournments, which, at the end of the day, serves no useful purpose than frustrating the victims.

The work of prosecutors can greatly affect the criminal justice system as a whole because prosecutors represent the key link between the state and correction systems. Addressing the needs of prosecutors could, therefore, contribute to improving the legitimacy and efficiency of our criminal justice system.

ADVOCATING A MODEL FOR MANAGING AND PREVENTING SEXUAL AND GENDER-BASED VIOLENCE (SGBV) AGAINST WOMEN AND GIRLS IN NIGERIA: AN OVERVIEW OF THE ACTIVITIES OF WOMEN AID COLLECTIVE (WACOL) WITH ITS STRATEGIC PARTNERS

By:
Ijeoma Chinaka Ezeude, LL.B, BL, LL.M

Head, Legal Unit, WACOL/Tamar SARC

Introduction

Women Aid Collective (WACOL) is an independent non-governmental, non-political and non-profit organisation formed under the visionary leadership of Prof. Joy Ngozi Ezeilo (OON) .The organisation is also registered with the Corporate Affairs Commission as a company limited by guarantee and as a charitable organisation with RC number (RC:388132), in 2000.[227]

The erudite scholar and founder of WACOL, Prof. Joy Ngozi Ezeilo, in her relentless quest for lasting solutions to issues bordering on Violence against Women and Girls (VAWG) and also on Sexual and Gender-Based Violence (SGBV) in Nigeria initiated the TAMAR SEXUAL ASSAULT AND REFERRAL CENTRE (TAMAR SARC) in 2014. The TAMAR SARC

---

[227] J.N. Ezeilo" Are we Born Free and Equal? Law, Justice and Human Rights" 144th Inaugural Lecture of the University of Nigeria, Delivered on Thursday, October 11, 2018, University of Nigeria Press, p.161.

is an entity managed in partnership with the Enugu State Ministries of Justice, Health, Gender Affairs and Social Development with funding from Justice For All/DFID United Kingdom. It is also a registered subsidiary of WACOL, focusing its work on rapid response and provision of integrated services, medical, legal, counselling, shelter, financial and psycho-social support for victims and survivors of sexual violence in Nigeria.[228]

Since its inception over twenty years ago, WACOL has rendered legal aid services to over sixty-five thousand women and young girls who are victims of different forms of Sexual and Gender-Based Violence (SGBV).The range of services rendered by WACOL are wide to wit; legal counselling, medical support, psycho-social support, financial assistance, shelter support, training, research, advocacy, intra-familial conflict resolution, capacity building, policy and advocacy reform, socio-political empowerment and library services.

WACOL / TAMAR SARC employ international best practices in responding to the needs of women and girls who are victims of sexual violence. In addition, WACOL has in the past, through its funding partners, facilitated a lot of groundbreaking activities to respond proactively to issues of Sexual and Gender-Based Violence. Some of the activities include; the domestic implementation of human rights, women's rights and then a children's rights project that trained hundreds of law enforcement agents – Police officers, civil defence officers, prosecutors, magistrates,high court judges and other administrators of justice – in Abia, Akwa-Ibom, Anambra, Ebonyi and Imo States on judicial application of human rights standards that are of special relevance to women and children in Nigeria. The organisation also pioneered paralegal trainings in Nigeria, and rule of law initiatives with focus on gender justice for women, one of which is the recent Police Conference training held on September 17th 2020 at Dannic Hotel, New Haven, Enugu.

These trainings are targeted at strengthening the capacities of law enforcement agents to respond rapidly and appropriately in cases of rape, defilement and other forms of violence especially against women and girls in Nigeria.

WACOL has conducted national and international research with over sixty publications pertaining to issues of women and children's rights.

---

[228] *Ibid.*p.161.

In the area of socio-political empowerment, WACOL has litigates human rights cases on behalf of women in Nigeria, builds the capacity of women and persons living with disabilities in leadership by increasing their participation and inclusion in politics. The CSO also educates youths on the menace of election violence among others.

In advocacy and policy reform, WACOL has drafted and reviewed a plethora of bills, participated in citizen's debate and submitted memoranda in the course of public hearings towards effective policy reforms; one of these is the Sexual Harassment Policy for Educational and Work Places in 2007. It also facilitated and pushed for the enactment of Violence against Persons Prohibition law in Enugu State in 2019 among other legislations.

WACOL Activities in Preventing Violence Against Women and Girls During Covid- 19 Pandemic As Supported By Its Partners.

In enhancing access to justice for women and girls who are victims of Sexual and Gender-Based Violence, WACOL has, through various projects, including the Women Voice and Leadership Project in partnership with Global Affairs Canada (GAC) and Action Aid Nigeria (AAN), continually rendered protective and integrated services to victims and survivors of SGBV. The range of integrated and protective services rendered by WACOL under the Women Voice and Leadership Project varies to wit; legal aid services, medical support, shelter support, psycho-social support and financial support.

Under the Legal Aid and Integrated services, victims are routinely offered legal counselling; cases presented are filed with relevant enforcement agencies to include police stations, and National Agency for Prohibition of Trafficking in Persons (NAPTIP) and where need be, in court, for trial of offenders. WACOL, through its legal team, *pro bono* lawyers and paralegal officers, ensure that there are appropriate filings, adequate routine monitoring and evaluation of cases, as well as urgent and emergency evacuation support of victims in cases of imminent or perceived danger or threat to life and security of the victim.

Good medical care is also given to victims under the medical support services, especially in cases of rape, defilement and other severe cases of assault occasioning grievous bodily harm. Victims are assisted with good medical treatments from government approved hospitals in Nigeria where forensic medical report crucial for police investigation and prosecution is prepared.

In the area of Shelter services, Prof .Joy Ezeilo, through WACOL, started the first shelter for women and girls in vulnerable situations in 1998 and built the first ever women's right group shelter for battered and abused women in 2001. WACOL, through its Shelter support and under the WVL project, provides adequate security, feeding, toiletries and necessities for women and girls who are victims and survivors of SGBV. Many victims and survivors have undergone psycho-social counselling by WACOL's team of psychologists who ensure at all times that traumatised victims, especially underage victims in rape, defilement, and other cases of violence requiring special psychological attention, undergo appropriate rehabilitation.

Financial assistance is also rendered to victims and survivors who are indigent and mostly come from rural communities, having no means of sustenance or livelihood.

In addition, WACOL, with support from funders, also works towards defending and responding rapidly to cases of infringement on the rights of women, children and young girls through technology driven services which have impacted greatly on the general public[229]. WACOL, through online services within the period of the Covid-19 pandemic, created a live chat on its website which allows victims to speak directly to counsellors. It also provided other online resources such as the legal literacy series (to educate people on VAWG/SGBV), survivors' forum and an e-version of survivors' newsletters. With these technological services, WACOL was able to receive and respond to the astronomical increase in violence against women during the Covid-19 pandemic. Also, under the WVL Project, WACOL produced and aired a jingle in English and Igbo languages. The jingle also created awareness on SGBV and the need to break the culture of silence and to report rape cases to WACOL and other relevant bodies that provide similar services.

At the peak of the Covid-19 lockdown and with the tremendous increase in violence against women and girls, WACOL, with support from partners,

---

[229] WACOL Press release available at https://www.independent.ng/we-receive-25-cases-of-rape-153-cases-of-domestic-violence-in-2-months-wacol/, accessed 15 October, 2020.

organised a successful protest to the Enugu State Police Command on the 5th of June, 2020 where a petition was handed to the Commissioner of Police calling for a state of emergency to be declared on rape. Also, WACOL led peaceful women protest marches against rape to the Enugu State Government House and Edo State Government House on the 18th and 19th of June 2020, respectively to raise public awareness on the scourge of rape and to call for the implementation of the Violence Against Persons Prohibition Law in the States[230].

Finally, WACOL received a total of two hundred and twenty-seven (227) cases of different forms of SGBV between April, May and June of 2020 during the Covid-19 lockdown and two hundred and twenty-nine cases (229) cases between July and September of the year 2020. The breakdown of these cases received and handled by WACOL before and during Covid-19 pandemic[231] together with the nature of violence and some spotlighted cases and the nature of assistance rendered by WACOL is highlighted hereunder.[232]

Table of summary of Thematic/Types of violations on SGBV for January, February and March, 2020, during Covid-19 pandemic lockdown

TYPES OF VAWG/NATURE OF CASE	Jan	Feb	Mar	QTR Total
Rape, defilement and Incest	0	3	2	5
Denial of Inheritance, Harmful widowhood practices, malicious damage to property	7	3	2	12
Physical and Emotional Abuses/Assaults	10	10	15	35
Trafficking, Child abuse	0	0	1	1
Forceful ejection and abandonment of spouse	3	5	15	23
Custody and Maintenance	10	4	3	17
Total	30	25	38	93

230 https://www.sunnewsonline.com/march-against-rape-in-enugu-part-of-nationwide-protests/om Yahoo Mail on Android https://www.sunnewsonline.com/march-against-rape-in-enugu-part-of-nationwide-protests/

231 Residents storm court as magistrate remands Enugu couple over abuse of 10-year-old maid see also Analysis: Kudos As WACOL Spearheads Justice for Tortured 10-Year-Old Maid | African Examiner, accessed October 16, 2020, https://m.facebook.com/story.php?story_fbid=1227588054255144&id=100010118838696&sfnsn=scwspmo&extid=cchgpuwMU8D4g6ds,

232 WACOL press release available at https://onlinebulletin.com.ng/2020/07/07/wacol-records-227-sexual-and-gender-based-violence-in-3-months/ accessed October 16, 2020.

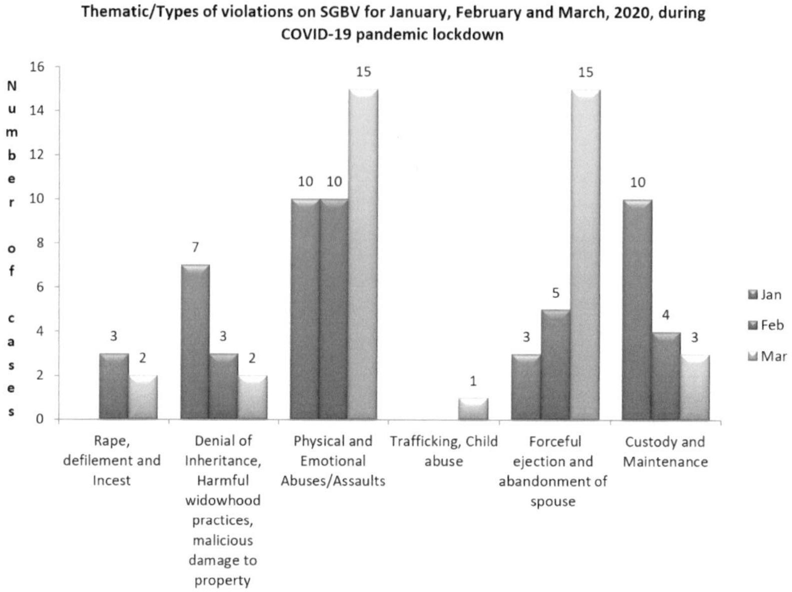

WACOL hotlines to report
+234 906 000 2128, +234 909 133 3000, +234 909 277 7000

Table of summary of Thematic/Types of violations on SGBV for April, May and June, 2020, during Covid-19 pandemic lockdown

TYPES OF VAWG/NATURE OF CASE	Apr	May	Jun	QTR Total
Rape, defilement and Incest	7	8	10	26
Denial of Inheritance, Harmful widowhood practices, malicious damage to property	2	1	2	5
Physical and Emotional Abuses, Assaults	32	28	37	97
Trafficking, Child abuse	0	0	2	2
Early forced marriage	0	1	1	2
Forceful ejection and abandonment of spouse	4	8	12	24
Discrimination on grounds of sex	1	0	2	3
Custody and Maintenance	32	16	20	68
Total	78	62	86	227

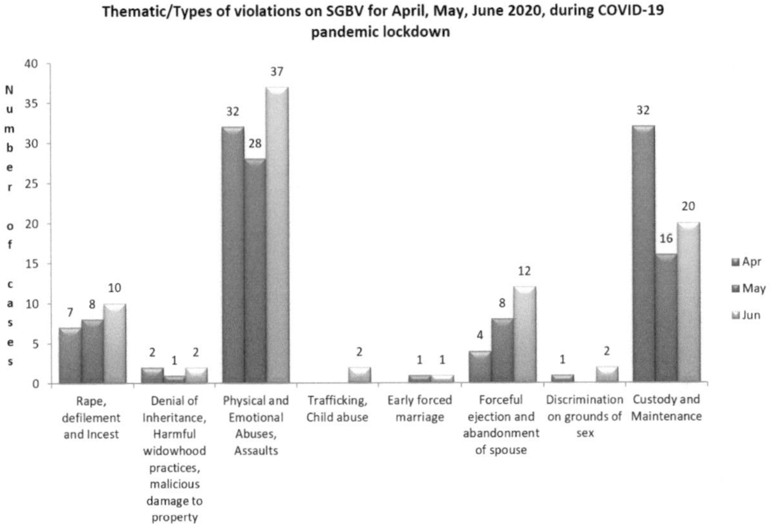

Table of summary of Thematic/Types of violations on SGBV for July, August, and September, 2020, during Covid-19 pandemic

TYPES OF VAWG/NATURE OF CASE	Jul-20	Aug-20	Sep-20
Rape, defilement and Incest	7	6	3
Denial of Inheritance, Harmful widowhood practices, malicious damage to property	1	18	4
Physical and Emotional Abuses/Assaults	31	32	24
Trafficking, Child abuse	2	3	2
Early forced marriage	1	0	1
Forceful ejection and abandonment of spouse	8	13	14
Custody and Maintenance	20	20	19
Total	70	92	67

Thematic/Types of violations on SGBV for July, August, and September, 2020, during COVID-19 pandemic

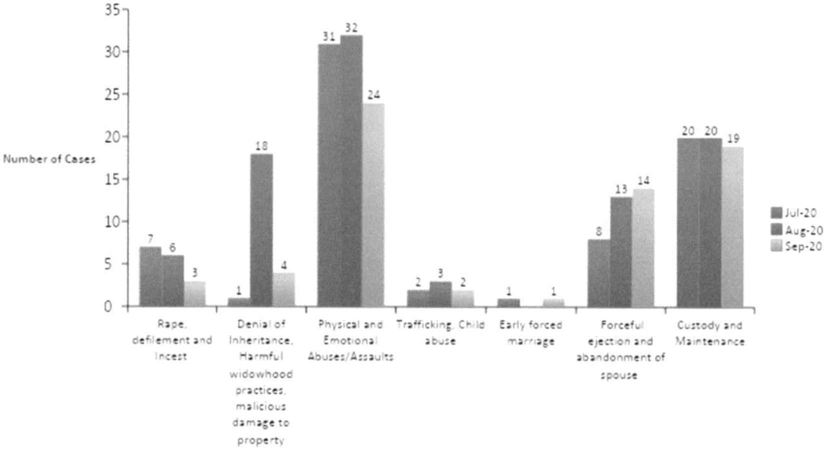

Table of summary of Thematic/Types of violations on SGBV for October, November and December, 2020, post Covid-19 pandemic lockdown

TYPES OF VAWG/NATURE OF CASE	Oct	Nov	Dec	QTR Total
Rape, defilement and Incest	1	4	3	8
Denial of Inheritance, Harmful widowhood practices, malicious damage to property	2	6	7	15
Physical and Emotional Abuses, Assaults	23	34	20	77
Trafficking, Child abuse	0	0	1	1
Early forced marriage	0	0	0	0
Forceful ejection and abandonment of spouse	13	11	5	29
Discrimination on grounds of sex	2	0	0	2
Custody and Maintenance	23	15	13	51
Total	64	70	49	183

Thematic/Types of violations on SGBV for October, November, December, 2020.

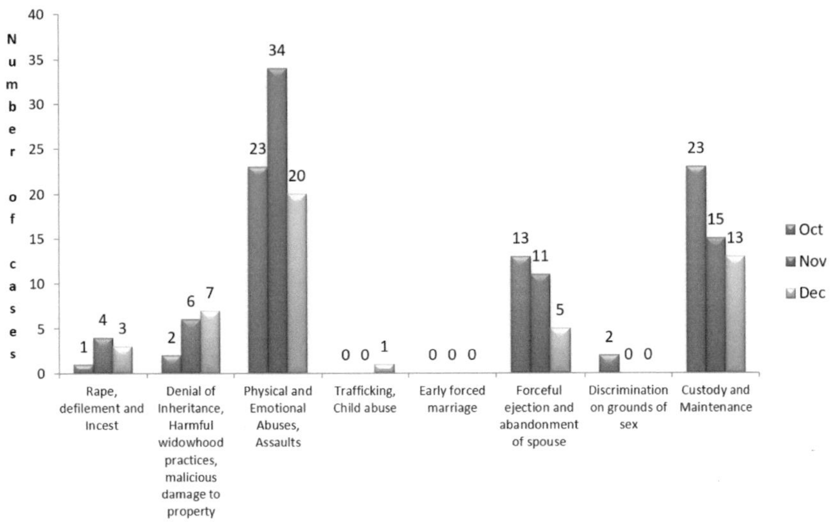

WACOL hotlines to report
+234 906 000 2128, +234 909 133 3000, +234 909 277 7000

Spotlighting of WACOL Cases

Case One. Abduction and Sexual Assault: On the 26th of April, 2020, WACOL received an emergency complaint of the case of a 13-year old girl who was abducted at gun point and sexually abused in the Abakpa Area of Enugu State. Immediately, WACOL, through its legal team activated the arrest of a hotel owner by the Abakpa Nike Police Division, Enugu, he is known for giving out his hotel rooms for use in serial defilement of underaged girls in the area. The victim was taken to a hospital for medical examination and treatment by WACOL. Police investigation is still ongoing in the matter and WACOL has given the victim the needed psycho-social support to enable her overcome the trauma.

Case Two. Defilement: One case of deep concern reported to WACOL during the period under review is the case of a 20-year old and mentally challenged girl from Iva Valley in Enugu, who was lured into an uncompleted building where she was sexually, abused resulting in pregnancy. On getting the report, WACOL aided the victim's guardian *ad litem* in apprehending the man responsible for the act, and committed him to taking care of the girl's ante natal/medical bills until she is delivered of the baby. The man has paid the first instalment of the bills in April and WACOL is following up on the matter accordingly.

Case Three. Emotional and Physical abuses/Assault: A 24-year old mother from Nnewi in Anambra State who had suffered multiple abuses in the hands of her husband was rescued by WACOL after she dropped a suicide note on her Facebook page. The victim was married off at the age of 15 years, has four children and stopped her secondary school education abruptly at SS1 when she got married. In addition, to being subjected to all manner of abuses, she suffered a medical condition known as Vesico Vagina Fistulae (VVF) and has been physically and emotionally abused by the husband because of her condition. The victim/survivor gladly received integrated assistance under the AAN/GAC, Covid -19 Top Up Grant that enabled her evacuation to Abuja where she had a surgery to correct her condition. WACOL paid for her transportation, accommodation and gave a *per diem* to sustain her while a good Samaritan, a Nollywood actress, who heard about her case from WACOL paid for the expensive surgery to correct the VVF condition. The surgery was successful. She consequently narrated to WACOL her success story of being able to control her urination. Meanwhile, her husband was arrested following a petition written to the Commissioner of Police Anambra State and subsequently released on bail. WACOL is still following up on the survivor for psycho-social support, counselling and livelihood sustainability.

Case Four. Physical Abuses/Assault: WACOL rescued a 24-year old breast feeding mother who was physically abused by her Ghanaian husband who also poured hot water on her two breasts. She was rushed to the hospital by WACOL. The victim/survivor, who sustained grievous bodily injuries on her two breasts, received proper medical treatment through WACOL medical support service. In narrating her ordeal, the victim/survivor stated that her husband had been in the habit of abusing her, on that very day he poured hot water on her two breasts because she demanded money for the family upkeep. The perpetrator was arrested upon a petition written to the Police and had been arraigned in court where the WACOL team, led by the Head of Legal, applied as *amicus* *curiae* and bail was vehemently refused and the perpetrator was further remanded.[233]

Case five. Defilement of a three year old minor: WACOL was alerted on the case of defilement of a three-year old minor on the 28th of August, 2020. The girl victim, who hails from Amofia Imezi Owa in Enugu state, was defiled by one Mr. Ismail from Kogi State, who happens to be a friend to the victim's family. The WACOL legal team immediately swung into action on receiving this information by reaching out to the IPO and OC, JWC in charge of the case at the 9th Mile Police Division, Enugu. In line with the instruction of the Commissioner of Police, the case, which was transferred to the State CID for further investigation, had been charged to court on the 4th of September, 2020. WACOL *pro bono* lawyers are following up relentlessly to make sure that Mr.Ismail faces the full wrath of the law for his act on the child victim. Also a medical report confirmed that the victim's hymen was ruptured. Meanwhile, the victim's distraught parents were provided with counseling support and the victim supported with good medical care and psycho-social support by WACOL.

Case Six. Disinheritance: A 51-year old widow from Enugu Ezike in Nsukka local government area who just lost her husband, called WACOL hotline to complain about threat to her life and attempt by her late husband's younger brother to dispossess her of the late husband's properties even when her late husband's corpse was still in the mortuary. WACOL intervened by calling her husband's younger brother who promised to maintain peace and accepted for WACOL to settle the matter amicably after the burial and lockdown.

Case 7. Welfare: A 32 year old woman reported that her husband batters her incessantly because of her request for welfare from him. The woman had recently given birth to a set of twin babies, and the husband refused to provide welfare and support for the family upkeep. Upon intervention, the man undertook to desist from battering the wife and also agreed to start providing welfare for the family, pending when WACOL resumes its physical operation to look into the other non emergency complaints from the couple.

---

233 https://guardian.ng/news/husband-pours-hot-water-on-nursing-wife-in-enugu/, http://www.africanexaminer.com/enugu-police-arrests-ghanaian-for-pouring-hot-water-on-wifes-chest-inflicting-serious-injuries/

Case Eight. Harmful / Obnoxious Traditional Practice: A 40-year old woman, a native of Ibagwa in Nsukka local government area and a mother of six children called that she is being threatened and accused of killing her co-wife's son. The woman is in a polygamous marriage and was asked to swear to an oath to deny the allegation that she was responsible for the death of her co-wife's son. On getting her distress call, WACOL called two representative heads of her family who participated in the family meeting where the decision was made against the woman and advised that they desist from such harmful traditional practice but rather to report to WACOL for settlement after the lockdown and they agreed.

Case 9. Rape: A report was received from a civil defence officer about a 21-year old girl who was raped on her way back from Church in a village called Ovoko in Nsukka Local government area of Enugu state. The victim was coming back from an Anglican church at the peak of the lockdown when she was accosted by the perpetrator who was unknown to her. The perpetrator forcefully dragged her and collected her phone. The victim, while struggling with the perpetrator over her phone, was overpowered, severely beaten up, weakened and raped by the perpetrator in a bushy path way. On getting this information, WACOL intervened immediately by moving to the location of the crime and taking pictures of the victim, including her torn clothes and blood stained underwear. WACOL also reported the matter to the Ibagwa Police Station which initiated investigations into the case. The victim was traumatised and in deep shock after the incident but was counselled by WACOL, after which she became stable and volunteered a statement to the police. The victim was also taken to a hospital where he was administered the necessary medical treatment and issued with a police medical report confirming rape. WACOL is following up on the police investigations and arrest of the culprit.

Women Aid Collective (WACOL) Online Survey on Sexual And Domestic Violence During Covid-19 Lockdown in Nigeria

Background / Context

The Corona Virus Disease (Covid-19) is one of the worst global pandemics with ravaging effects on the global community. The outbreak of the virus came with different global measures put in place so as to help contain the spread of the virus. Some of these measures include the regular washing of hands, hand sanitizing, use of face masks/shield, social distancing, lockdown of businesses and stay-at-home policy. The peak of the pandemic, coupled with the stay-at home policy and lockdown of businesses in Nigeria witnessed an astronomical rise in cases of Sexual and Gender- Based Violence, especially against women and girls. The rise in cases of violence against women and girls is evidenced in various reported incidents of violencc across Nigeria. Joy Ngozi Ezeilo[234] raised an alarm on the need to avert exacerbation of SGBV within families during the lockdown. In her words: "the world must respond promptly to avoid exacerbation of pandemic upon another pandemic of Sexual and Gender-Based Violence (SGBV)". She further stressed, in a press statement during the pandemic, that: "it is becoming clearer that we are not just fighting the Corona virus pandemic in Nigeria but also the rape epidemic happening upon the Covid-19 pandemic"[235]. On May 31st, a University of Benin undergraduate student was gang raped in a church and murdered in cold blood; on the 26th June, the Katsina State Police Command reported the arrests of 40 suspects within this period of Covid-19 lockdown (between April and June 2020); and on 24th June, the Akwa Ibom State Police Command arrested a pastor and eleven others for rape and defilement.[236] Within these months of April to June of Covid-19 lockdown, WACOL received and handled two hundred and twenty-seven (227) cases of Sexual and Gender Based-Violence. Out of these 227 cases, twenty-five of these cases bordered on rape, incest, defilements, and sexual assaults of underage girls.

It is against this background, that Women Aid Collective (WACOL) conducted an online survey with a view to finding out the major causes of the spike in cases of Sexual and Gender-Based Violence during the lockdown, especially against women and girls, so as to proffer workable solutions for effective policy formulation in Nigeria.

---

234 Prof. Joy Ezeilo, Prof of law, Dean Emeritus of the Faculty of Law, University of Nigeria, Enugu Campus, she is the Founder/Executive Director of Women Aid Collective (WACOL)/ Tamar Referral Centre (TAMAR SARC), Enugu, Nigeria, Human Rights Defender Award winner, 2019, in a live broadcast on "Covid-19 Pandemic and the Spike in Violence Against Women and Girls in Nigeria" at Solid FM 100.9 on the 25th of April, 2020.

235 Prof Joy Ngozi Ezeilo " Rape and the Law in Nigeria: Blaming Stigmatization and Silencing victims in Search of Justice", available at https//www.thisdaylive.com/index-php/2020/06/30/the- rape-scourge

236 *Ibid.*

METHODOLOGY

The legal clinic of Women Aid Collective (WACOL) during Covid-19 pandemic designed an online survey to find out the opinions of the global community on the causes of the spike in Sexual and Gender-Based Violence (SGBV) and to proffer effective and workable policy formulation for the country. All survey questionnaires were distributed via different online platforms to wit; WhatsApp pages, Twitter handles, Facebook, Emails, and Instagram among others. The six geo-political zones in Nigeria were proportionately represented as well as the six continents of the world. A total of four hundred and twenty-three responses (423) were gathered and errors were minimal.

A pilot survey of twenty (20) persons was done to ascertain their various opinions on the subject before the final circulation. This pilot survey was not included in the final data set. Analysis was done using percentages, charts and tables.

Descriptive Statistics of age of respondents (N, 423)

	Min	Max	M	SD
Age of respondents	18	77	37.8	11.1

Age of respondents in groups (N, 423)

	Frequency	Percent
18-24 years	46	10.9
25-34 years	131	31.0
35-44 years	141	33.3
45-59 years	85	20.1
60 years and above	20	4.7

Description of respondents according to their age. The chart above shows that 10.9% are between ages 18-24; 31.0% between ages 25-35; 33.3% between ages 35-44; 20.1% of respondents are in age range 45-59 while 4.7% of them are aged 60 years and above. Findings reveals that age range 35-44 years had the highest number of respondents while 60 years and above had the lowest.

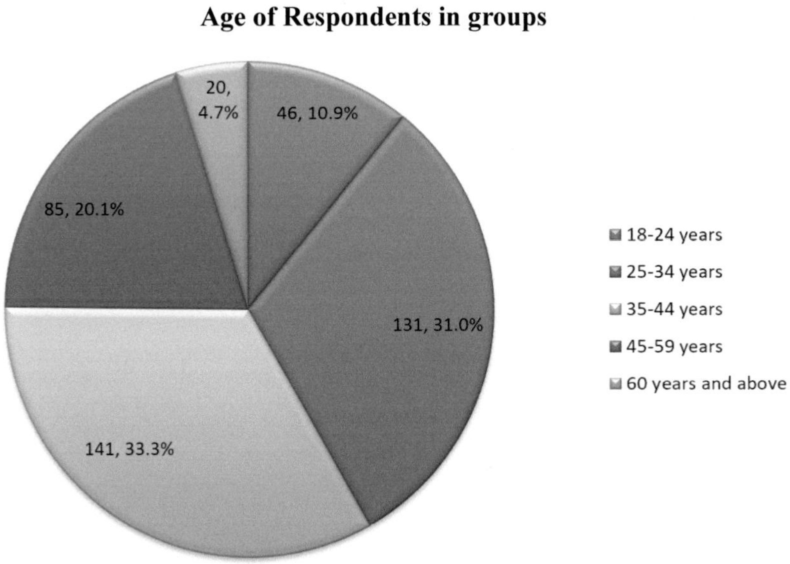

Gender of respondents (N, 423)

	Frequency	Percent
Male	145	34.3
Female	278	65.7

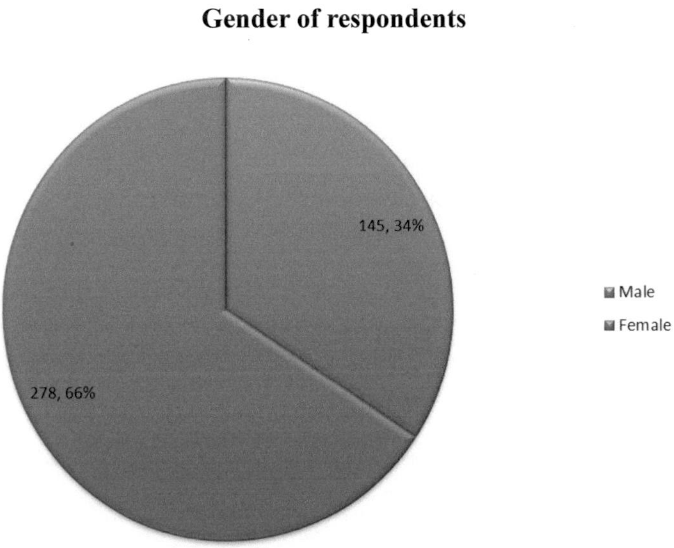

From the diagram above, the female respondents make up 66% of the whole while the male respondent make up 34%. What this reveals is that females responded more than males to the survey.

Marital status (N, 423)

	Frequency	Percent
Single	143	33.8
Married	251	59.3
Separated	15	3.5
Divorced	3	.7
Widow/Widower	11	2.6

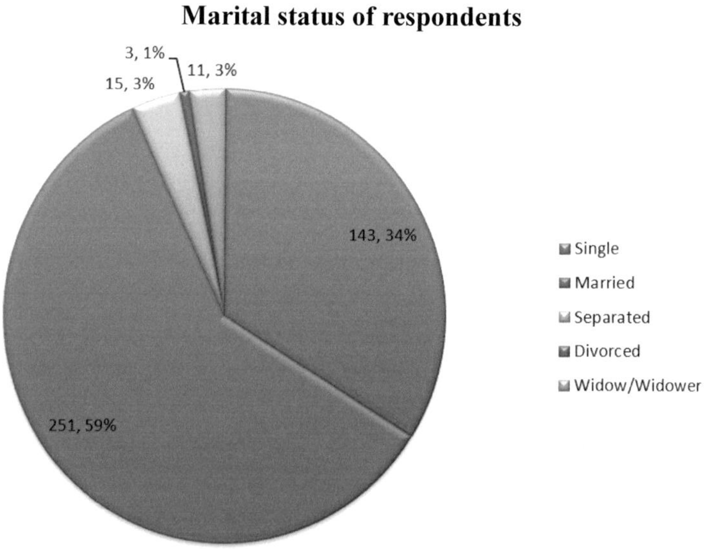

The chart above summarises the marital status of the respondents as follows: 33.8% of respondents that participated in the survey are single, 59.3% are married, 3.5% are separated, 7% are divorced while 2.6% are widowers/ widows. These figures reveal that the highest responses came from those that are married.

Occupation of respondents (N, 397)

	Frequency	Percent
Clergy	2	0.5
Artisan	3	0.8
Private sector	4	1
Self-employed	5	1.3
Medical workers	5	1.3
Unemployed	7	1.8
Trader	11	2.8
Lawyer/Legal practitioner	14	3.5
Teacher	32	8.1
Business	45	11.3
Student	57	14.4
Public servant	94	23.7
Civil servant	118	29.7

On the occupation of respondents, 0.5 % are clergy; 0.8% are artisans; 1% private are sector workers; 1.3% are self-employed,1.3% are medical workers, 1.8% are unemployed; 2.8% are traders, 3% are lawyers/legal practitioners; 8.1% are teachers; 11.3% are businessmen and women,14.4% are students; 23.7% are public servants; and 29.7% are civil servants.

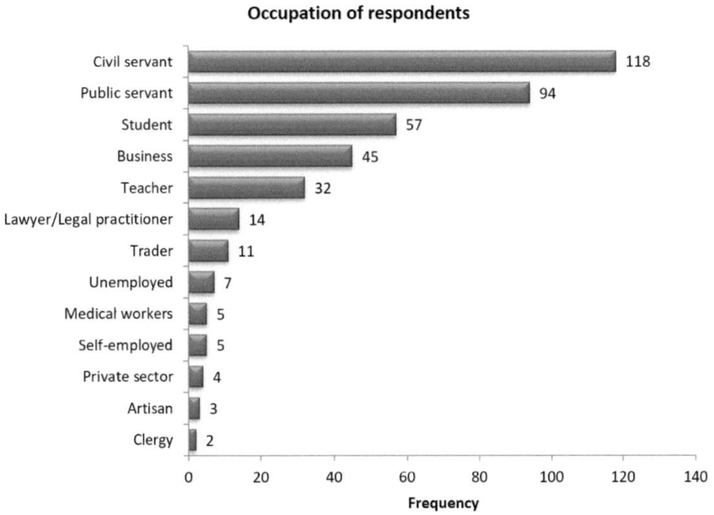

Location of respondents (N, 423)

	Frequency	Percent
Europe	2	0.5
America	5	1.2
Africa	6	1.4
South-south, Nigeria	35	8.3
North-west, Nigeria	49	11.6
South-west, Nigeria	62	14.7
North-central, Nigeria	65	15.4
South-east, Nigeria	199	47

On the location of respondents, 0.5% are in Europe; 1.2% are in America; 1.4% are in Africa; 8.3% are in South Nigeria; 11.6% are in North West Nigeria; 14.7% are in South West Nigeria; 15.4% are in North Central Nigeria; and 47% are in South East Nigeria. From the chart, the location with the highest number of responses is South East Nigeria

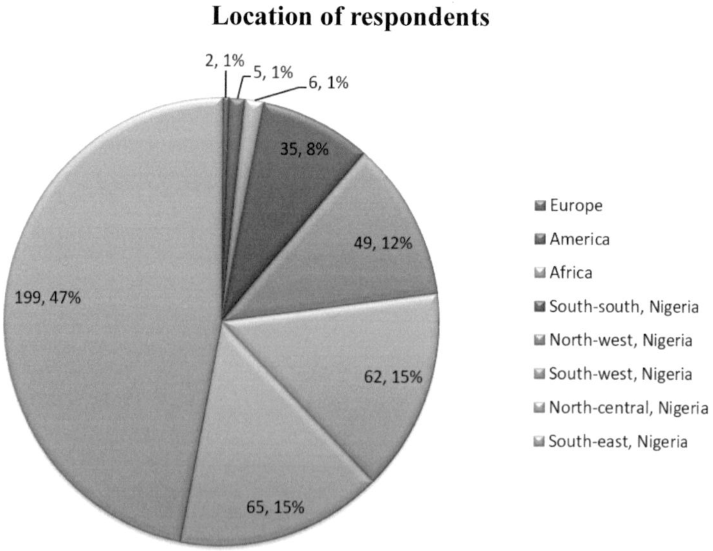

Pattern of Knowledge of types of Sexual and Gender-Based Violence (SGBV) by respondents. (N, 423)

	Average scores
Economic violence	.54
Harmful traditional practices	.64
Mental/Emotional violence	.78
Sexual violence	.86
Physical violence	.86

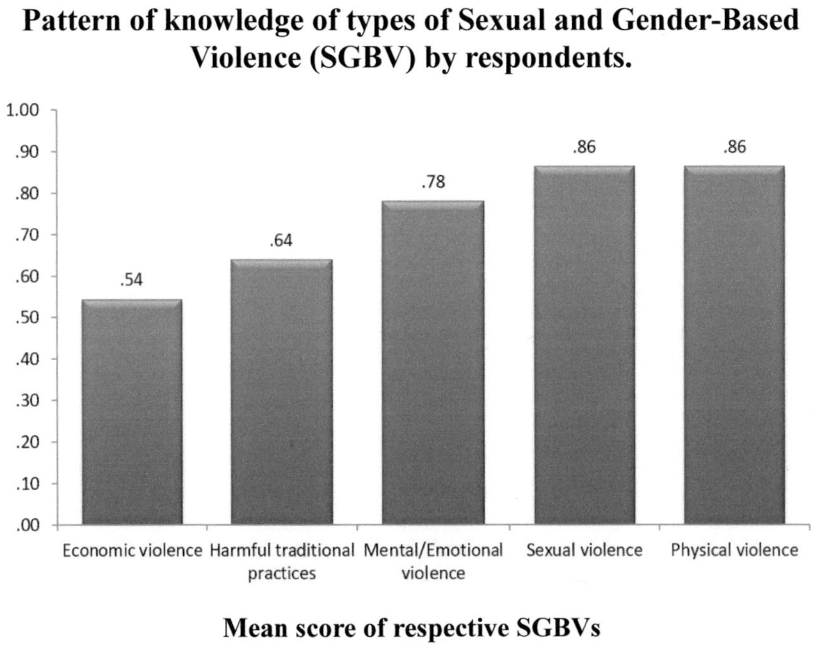

Whether respondents are victims or know any victim of SGBV (N, 423)

	Frequency	Percent
Yes	277	65.5
No	146	34.5

From the chart above, the number of respondents who are victims of SGBV or know anybody who is a victim is 65.5% while the number of respondents who are not victims or do not know anyone who is a victim is 34.5%. This shows that majority of the respondents have either been victims of violence or known victims of violence.

Knowledge of anyone you suffered from any form of Sexual and Gender-Based Violence (SGBV)?

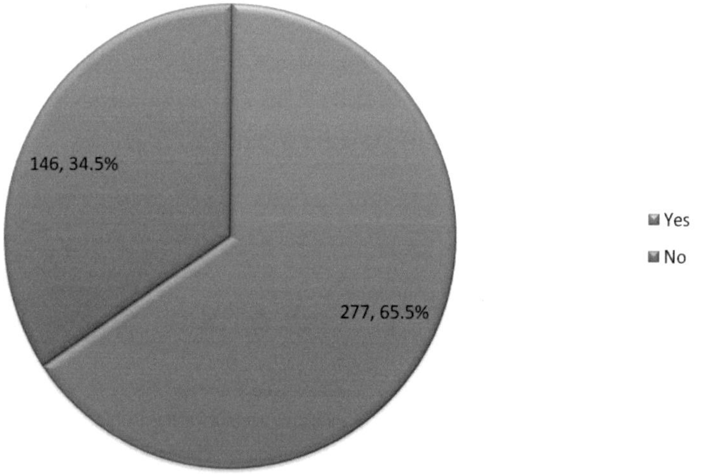

Types of Sexual and Gender-Based Violence (SGBV) experienced by respondents or persons they know during Covid-19 lockdown. (N, 423)

	Average scores
Cyber/internet/online stalking	.02
Female circumcision or genital mutilation	.02
Early/forced marriage	.03
Denial of inheritance	.03
Harmful widowhood practices	.04
Unwanted invasion of privacy.	.10
Intimidation	.10
Any threat to violence	.12

Indecent assault	.12
Sexual harassment	.13
Abandonment	.14
Defilement	.14
Push, biting, kicking, slapping, pulling of hair, using harmful objects etc to cause injury	.16
Forceful ejection from home	.17
None provision of welfare	.25
Rape	.27
Verbal abuse or discrimination	.35

Types of Sexual and Gender-Based Violence (SGBV) experienced by respondents or persons they know during COVID-19 lockdown.

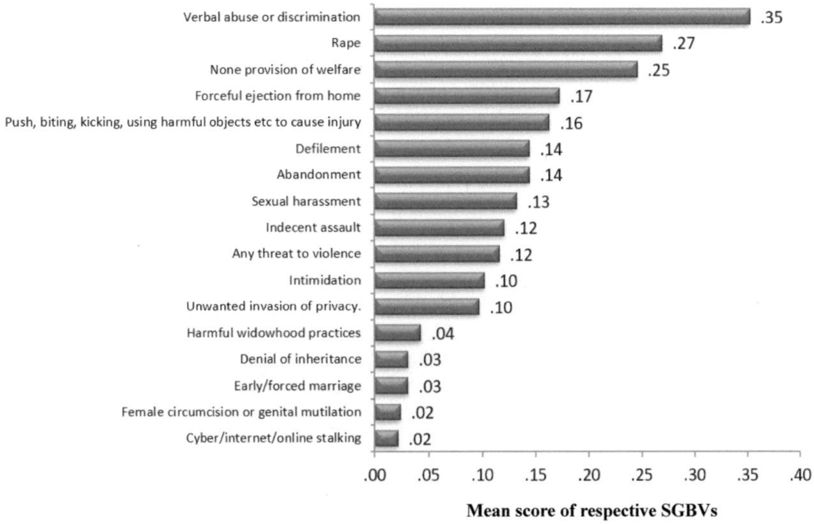

From the above chart, the type of Sexual and Gender-Based Violence experienced by the majority of respondents during the Covid-19 lockdown is verbal abuse and discrimination while Cyber/Internet/online stalking is the least experienced violence during the lockdown by the respondents.

Pattern of relationship between the perpetrators of Sexual and Gender-Based Violence (SGBV) with the victims. (N, 268)

	Frequency	Per cent
Others	6	2.2
Religious leader	7	2.6
Law enforcement officer	9	3.4
Boyfriend/Girl friend	19	7.1
Household member	26	9.7
Family member	29	10.8
Village/community member	32	11.9
Stranger/unknown person	36	13.4
Husband/Wife	104	38.8

On the pattern of relationship between victims and perpetrators of Sexual and Gender-Based Violence, 2.2% of the respondents answered 'others'; 2.6% of respondents ticked 'Religious leader'; 3.4% chose 'Law enforcement officer'; 7.1% ticked 'Boyfriend/Girl Friend'; 9.7% chose 'Household member'; 10.8% marked relationship as 'family member'; 11.9% ticked 'Village/Community Leader'; 13.4% went through a violent ordeal in the hands of 'Stranger/ Unknown Person'; while 38.8% marked 'Husband/wife'. The respondents' answer in the area of the relationship between the perpetrator and the victim is higher in case of husband and wife.

Pattern of relationship between the perpetrators of Sexual and Gender-Based Violence (SGBV) with the victims

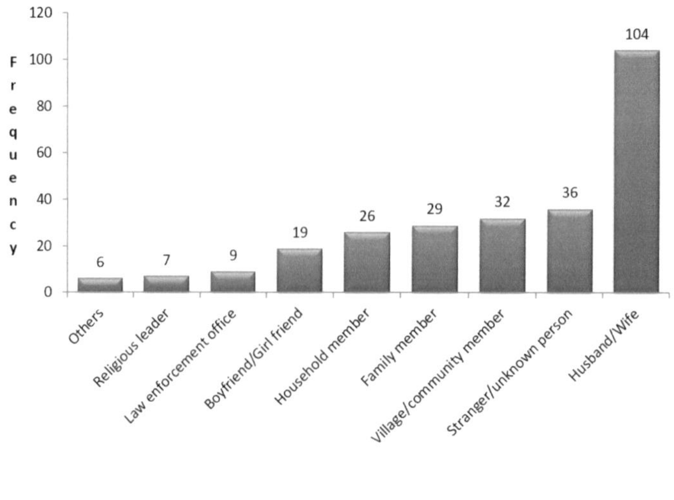

Gender of abuser (N, 262)

	Frequency	Percent
Male	205	78.2
Female	57	21.8

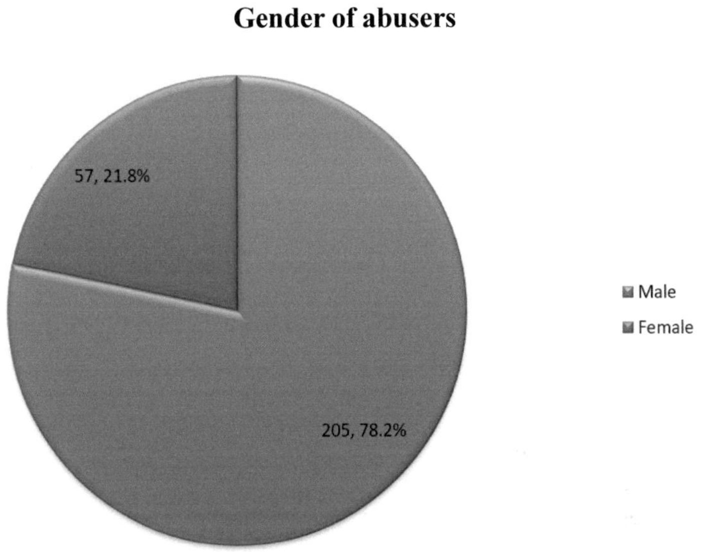

On Gender of abusers 78% of the respondents ticked 'males' while 21.8% of the respondents picked 'females' as abusers. This shows that majority of SGBV perpetrators are males.

Pattern of immediate cause of the SGBVs. (N, 248)

	Frequency	Percent
Work-related problems	10	4
Custody and child support	12	4.8
Others	15	6
Food and family problems	18	7.3
Jealousy	19	7.7

Substance abuse	20	8.1
Adultery	26	10.5
Disrespect	38	15.3
Financial problem	90	36.3

On pattern of immediate cause of SGBV, the chart shows work related, 4%; custody and child support, 4.8%; others, 6%; food and family problems, 7.3 %; jealousy, 7.7%; substance abuse, 8.1%; adultery, 10.5%; disrespect, 15%; and financial problem, 36.3%. This chart reveals that the respondents identified the major cause of SGBV as being 'financial problem'.

Pattern the immediate cause of the SGBVs.

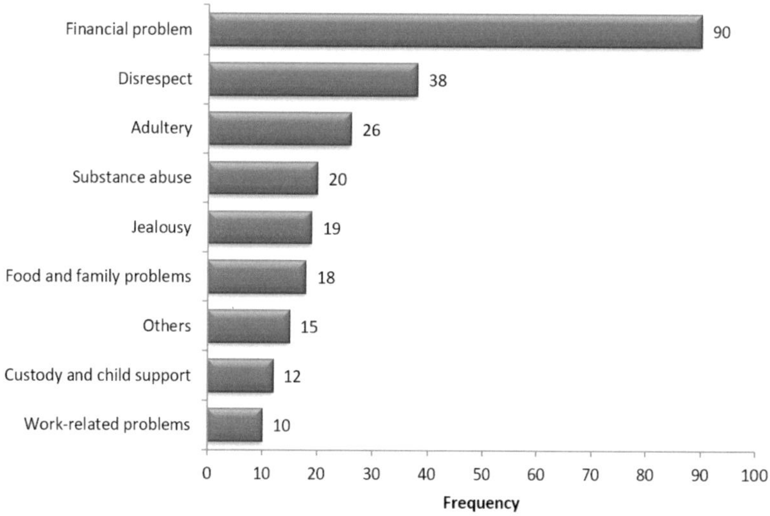

Whether the SGBV was reported. (N, 268)

	Frequency	Percent
Yes	98	36.6
No	124	46.3
Don't know	46	17.2

On whether the SGBV was reported, 36.6% of the respondents answered 'Yes'; 46.3% answered 'No'; while the other 17.2 % ticked 'Don't Know'. This chart reveals that majority of the respondents answered 'No', meaning that the majority of the SGBV cases are not reported.

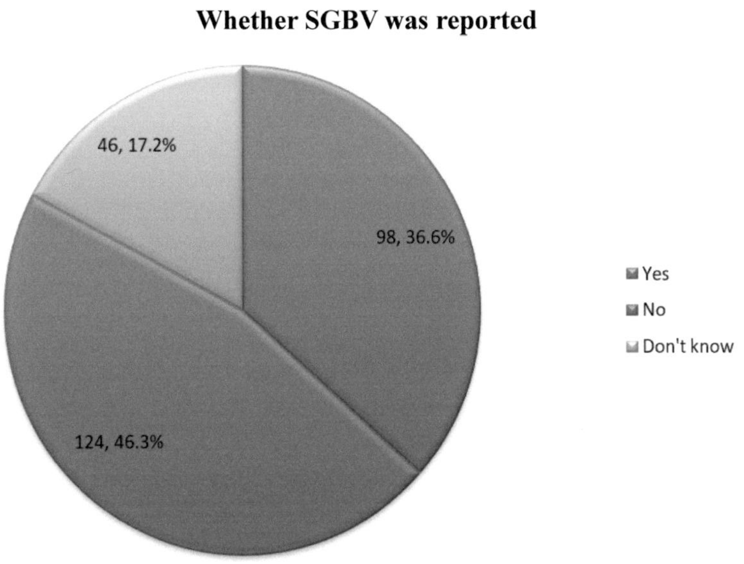

To who reported? (N, 163)

	Frequency	Percent
Religious leader	8	4.9
Community leader	12	7.4
CSO/NGO	42	25.8
Don't know	47	28.8
Law enforcement officer	44	27.0
Neighbourhood/family	10	6.1
Total	163	100.0

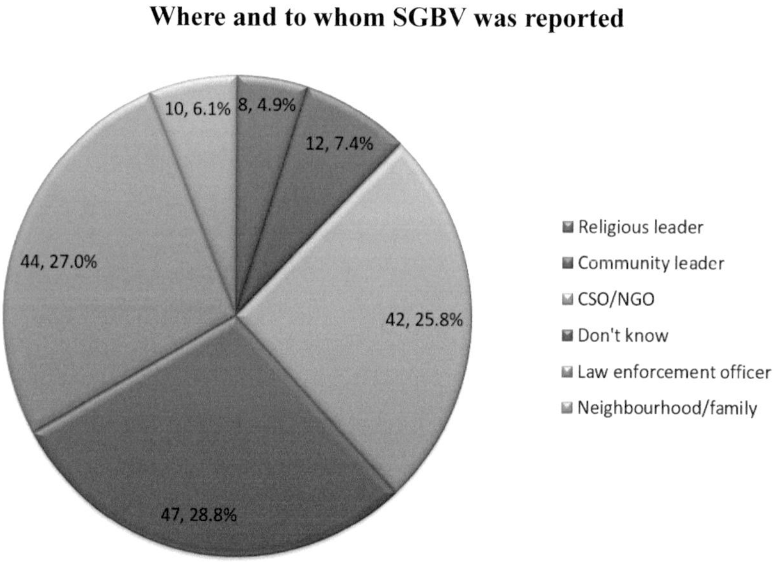

From the above chart, 4.9% of the respondents answered that cases of violence were reported to Religious Leaders; 7.4%, Community leaders; 25.8%, CSO/NGO; 28.8%, Don't Know; 27.0%, Law Enforcement Officer; and 6.1%, Neighbourhood/family. The percentage of respondents who do not know whether the cases were reported is the highest.

Pattern of suggested remedies to mitigate Sexual and Gender Based-Violence (SGBV) during Covid-19 lockdown. (N, 423)

	Average scores
Psycho-social support services for victims/survivors	1.86
Medical support to victims/survivors.	1.89
Free legal and counselling services to victims/survivors.	1.90
Help women to be economically independent.	1.95
Shelter support services to victims/survivors.	1.97
Make penalties for SGBVs consistent, proportional and firm.	2.00
Naming and shaming the perpetrators.	2.12
Media exposure of perpetrators, phone hotline, social media (WhatsApp, Facebook, etc)	2.13

Increase funding for support services.	2.15
Good communication among family members.	2.20
Good understanding of the Covid-19 pandemic.	2.57
Palliative from government, organisations and neighbours	2.69

On the pattern of suggested remedies to mitigate SGBV, the frequency of responses is highest in the area of Government, Organisations and Neighbours providing palliatives while psycho-social support services for victims/survivors have the least number of responses.

Pattern of suggested remedies to mitigate Sexual and Gender-Based Violence (SGBV) during COVID-19 lockdown.

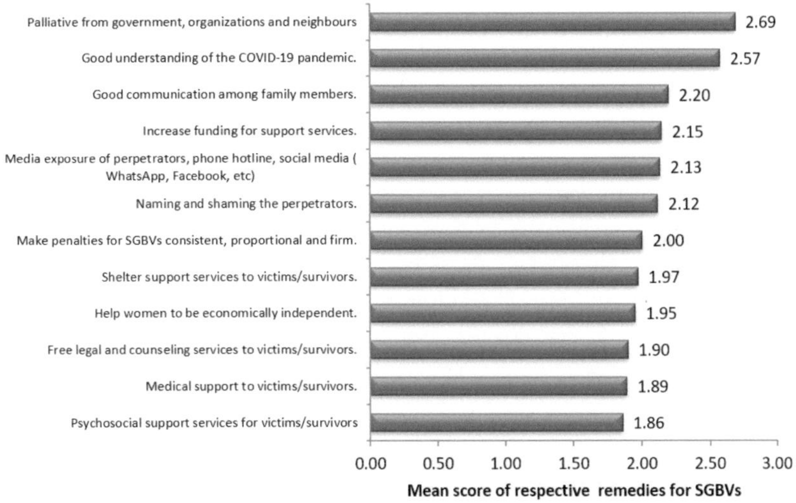

Conclusion

WACOL, from inception, has remained in the forefront of protection of women's, girls' and children's rights in Nigeria and beyond. Its proactive and responsive efforts in protecting victims of SGBV during the Covid-19 pandemic lockdown remains commendable and a landmark achievement in the organisation's bid for a better society.The achievements of WACOL so far in receiving and handling over four hundred and fifty-six (456) cases of SGBV between the months of April to September 2020, with support from its strategic partners underscore the enormous potentials in the non-governmental organisations and the development sector's capabilities in providing solutions in the area of SGBV.

This success indices re-emphasise the need for more concerted inter-sectoral and multi-sectoral collaborative efforts among major stakeholders in addressing the scourge of SGBV in Nigeria. The government as a major stakeholder in the SGBV project should form stronger synergy with the CSO's and NGO's through strategic policy formulation, policy drive and implementation, as well adequate funding, if the country's dream of an SGBV-free society can be attained.

ENUGU STATE VIOLENCE AGAINST PERSONS (PROHIBITION) LAW 2019 AS A SUCCOUR TO WOMEN: REVISITING THE POLEMIC REGARDING FEMALE GENITAL RITUAL

Dr. Obiajulu Nnamuchi

Oppressed women typically want their rights as individuals to be secured within their own culture, not at the expense of exile from their culture, or the destruction of what they and others take to be valuable about their culture.

– Amy Gutmann,
Human Rights as Politics and Idolatry, 2001

Abstract

The recent enactment of the Violence Against Persons (Prohibition) (VAPP) Law in Enugu State was widely heralded as signaling seriousness on the part of lawmakers to finally rein in perpetrators of human rights abuses on women in the state. The tentacles of the law are quite vast, proscribing obnoxious traditions such as harmful widowhood practices and redefining certain proscriptions (rape, for instance) in tandem with current global realities. Indeed, whilst undeniable that the statute, in many respects, represents a legitimate advancement of human rights, some of its provisions are shrouded in controversy. An instance of the latter is the section outlawing female circumcision or female genital ritual (FGR). Obviously, the legislators that crafted the legal framework as well as their supporters in the human rights community are of the mindset that criminalising FGR is consistent with protecting women from the "violence" said to be represented by the procedure. Whilst this position holds true in some cases, in others, the reverse would be the case—for instance, regarding consenting women. The question then becomes, should the procedure, when performed on these women, be subjected to the same sanction as those forced on non-consenting ones or, for that matter, sanctioned at all? Should the VAPP Law of Enugu State make such distinction? Responding to these questions is the task of this paper.

I. INTRODUCTION

Despite its title being couched in a neutral language, a close reading of the Violence Against Persons (Prohibition) (VAPP) Law 2019 of Enugu State would readily betray the intention of the piece of legislation, namely, elimination of gender-based violence, specifically the kind perpetrated against women. This is, no doubt, a noble goal; nonetheless, although freedom from violence is enshrined as a human right in a gamut of municipal and international human rights regimes, the stark reality is that this is amongst the most violated of all human rights, affecting all demographics and socio-economic strata, particularly women. That explains the recent emergence of violence against women and girls (VAWG)[237] as an important concern of the international community. VAWG—defined as "any act of violence that results in, or is likely to result in, physical, sexual, mental or economic harm to women, including threats of such acts, coercion or arbitrary deprivation of liberty, whether occurring in public or in private life"[238] — is encapsulated within the concern of the VAPP Law of Enugu State. Virtually all forms of violence targeted for extinction by the VAPP Law are included within the definition of VAWG, such as intimate partner violence; rape and sexual assault (including as a tactic of war); female genital mutilation; child, early or forced marriage; trafficking of women for labour or sexual exploitation; accusations of witchcraft; denial of economic resources as a means to exert control ('economic abuse'); street or cyber harassment; and violations of sexual and reproductive health and rights, such as denial of access to

[237] Actionaid, *Ending violence against women and girls (VAWG)*, available at https://www.actionaid.org.uk/our-work/policy-and-research/ending-violence-against-women-and-girls (accessed 5 September 2020).

[238] *Id.*

safe abortion.[239] Whilst the scourge of violence is a global phenomenon, prevalence varies in tandem with the degree of unequal power relationships and access to resources, the result being that residents of impoverished third world countries, especially women, are disproportionately impacted *vis-à-vis* their contemporaries in more affluent societies. These (the former) are countries where neither civil and political rights nor economic, social and cultural rights are respected, at least, not to the same extent as in Western democracies. Nigeria is infamously amongst the third world countries.

Described as "violence that is directed against a woman because she is a woman or that affects women disproportionately,"[240] gender-based violence is "a form of discrimination that seriously inhibits women's ability to enjoy rights and freedoms on a basis of equality with men."[241] The effect is to impair or nullify women's enjoyment of human rights and fundamental freedoms enshrined in international and domestic human rights regimes.[242] These are acts that "inflict physical, mental or sexual harm or suffering, threats of such acts, coercion and other deprivations of liberty"[243] such as those inspired by cultural attitude by which women are accorded inferior status including, but not limited to, forced marriage, dowry deaths, acid attacks and female circumcision.[244] An equivalent definition is housed in section 2 of the Enugu State VAPP Law, which defines harmful traditional practices to include "all traditional behaviour, attitudes and/or practices, which negatively affect the fundamental rights of women, girls, or any person and includes harmful widowhood practices," as well as "denial of inheritance or succession rights, female genital mutilation or female circumcision, forced marriage and forced isolation from family and friends."

To accentuate the status of female circumcision or female genital ritual (FGR) as an instance of "harmful traditional practices", section 9 (1) of the VAPP Law

239 *Id.*

240 Committee on the Elimination of Discrimination against Women, General Recommendation 19, Violence against women (Eleventh session, 1992), 6, U.N. Doc. A/47/38 at 1 (1993), reprinted in Compilation of General Comments and General Recommendations Adopted by Human Rights Treaty Bodies, U.N. Doc. HRI/GEN/1/Rev.6 at 243 (2003).

241 *Id.* 1.

242 *Id.* 7, 11.

243 *Id.* 6.

244 *Id.* 11.

proscribes the practice regardless of whether a girl child or woman is affected. And this is the crux of the problem. In imposing a blanket ban on FGR, the statutory framework fails to draw a distinction between the willing and coerced. Although it might appear implausible that some women would willingly submit themselves to FGR, the reality, as would become evident shortly, is, in fact, different. Regarding these people, so long as they are mature rational adults whose competence to make decisions for themselves are not compromised in any discernible way, to subject their decision to criminal prosecution can be challenged (as Part IV demonstrates) as a human rights violation.

This paper consists of five sections. Following this introductory section, Part II explores the terms "circumcision," "mutilation," "cutting" and "ritual"—all of which have been used in description of FGR—and their appropriateness or otherwise. Equally discussed in the section are the four severity-based categorisations of FGR. In Part III, the paper examines the claim that FGR harbours a legion of adverse health consequences, and whether this claim can be substantiated. Part IV argues that autonomy or the right to self-determination shields consenting women from FGR-related sanctions. In Part V—the Conclusion—the paper advocates toleration, for accommodation of views and actions that deviate from the mainstream, such as those by women that voluntarily submit themselves to FGR.

II. NOMENCLATURE, TYPES OF FEMALE GENITAL RITUAL AND SOUTHEASTERN NIGERIA

Nomenclature is very important in the sense that the term used to describe an event or action often determines responses to that event or action, explaining why the terms "female circumcision" or "genital mutilation" used in section 9(1) of the VAPP Law of Enugu State elicit debate amongst scholars as well as activists and the general populace. Whilst some approve of one of the terms and repudiate the other, others invent completely new ones. For some, the term "female cutting" is preferable in the sense that it appears neutral and less offensive to people in practicing societies.[245] Two authors advocate the use of three terms, namely, "female genital cutting" ("FGC"), "female circumcision,"

---

[245] See, for instance, REBECCA J. COOK, BERNARD M. DICKENS AND MAHMOUD F. FATHALLA, REPRODUCTIVE HEALTH AND HUMAN RIGHTS: INTEGRATING MEDICINE, ETHICS AND LAW 263 (2003).

and "female genital surgery," and reject using "female genital mutilation" (FGM) which they consider inflammatory.[246] The word "mutilation", notes legal scholar, Makau Mutua, "implies the willful, sadistic infliction of pain on a hapless victim, and stigmatises the practitioners and their culture as barbaric savages."[247] Whilst this characterisation might appeal to eradication activists, same cannot be said of FGR practitioners.

The dichotomy between FGM and the various other alternative terms needs to be contextualised in terms of the novelty of the former. Not quite long ago, the universal term, even in medical literature, was female cutting, but increasingly the use is being jettisoned in favour of FGM. This preference is said to be based on the idea that describing the procedure as female cutting falsely analogises FGM to male circumcision, thereby confusing two remarkably distinct practices.[248] FGM is said to more aptly capture the gruesome and harmful nature of the act and, more importantly, recasts it more concretely as a human rights violation, thereby providing a more robust ground upon which to campaign for its abolition.[249] Casting FGM as a human rights violation removes the practice from the arena of culture (and its attendant legitimacy) and makes it more susceptible to objective moral criticism.

The nomenclature "FGM" was adopted in 1990 at the third conference of the Inter-African Committee on Traditional Practices Affecting the Health of Women and Children (IAC)—an international non-governmental organisation based in Dakar, Senegal—held in Addis Ababa, Ethiopia. Following WHO's recommendation in 1991 that the United Nations (U.N.) adopt this term,[250] its use has quickly spread like wild fire, embraced, not only by the organisation

---

[246]Nancy Ehrenreich & Mark Barr, *Intersex Surgery, Female Genital Cutting, and the Selective Condemnation of 'Cultural Practices* 40 (1) HARVARD CIVIL RIGHTS-CIVIL LIBERTIES LAW REVIEW 71, 72, note 4 (2005).

[247] MAKAU MUTUA, HUMAN RIGHTS: A POLITICAL AND CULTURAL CRITIQUE 26 (2002).

[248] WHO, *Eliminating Female Genital Mutilation: An Interagency Statement* UNAIDS, UNDP, UNECA, UNESCO, UNFPA, UNHCHR, UNHCR, UNICEF, UNIFEM, WHO 2 (2008); MARTHA NUSSBAUM, SEX AND SOCIAL JUSTICE 119 (1999).

[249] WHO *id.*

[250] UNICEF, *Changing a Harmful Social Convention: Female Genital Mutilation/Cutting*, Innocenti Digest, 2005, at 2, available at https://www.unicef-irc.org/publications/pdf/fgm eng.pdf (accessed 5 September 2020).

and its agencies, but also a plurality of scholars and civil society groups pushing one agenda or the other. Thus, in employing the term "genital mutilation" the drafters of VAPP Law of Enugu State was following the 1990 recommendation of the WHO, even if unwittingly. This paper adopts the term "FGR" because it is neutral, non-condemnatory and captures the ritualistic dimension of the practice.

The WHO defines FGR as consisting of all procedures involving partial or total removal of the external female genitalia, or other injury to the female genital organs for non-therapeutic reasons.[251] They are of four types. Type 1 is the partial or total removal of the clitoral glans (the external and visible part of the clitoris, which is a sensitive part of the female genitals), and/or the prepuce/ clitoral hood (the fold of skin surrounding the clitoral glans). Type 2 refers to the partial or total removal of the clitoral glans and the *labia minora* (the inner folds of the vulva), with or without removal of the *labia majora* (the outer folds of skin of the vulva). Type 3, which is also known as infibulation, involves the narrowing of the vaginal orifice through the creation of a covering seal. The seal is formed by cutting and repositioning the *labia minora*, or *labia majora*, sometimes through stitching, with or without removal of the clitoral prepuce/clitoral hood and glans (Type I FGM). All other harmful procedures to the female genitalia for non-medical purposes are classified as Type 4 and includes pricking, piercing, incising, scraping and cauterising the genital area.

Although the categorisation or classification is premised on varying levels of severity, all of them are deemed to be mutilation and proscribed. As to whether the blanket ban is justifiable or whether it is right to attach "mutilation" to all forms of FGR, Nowa Omoigui, a Nigerian cardiologist practicing in the United States, argues that there is a "huge difference between Circumcision and Mutilation" and to "group all forms of age old religious circumcision into one large category under the guise of medical enlightenment and 'civilization' is very unfortunate."[252] Describing the term FGM as "mischievous and hypocritical," he elucidates, in reference to his native Edo State:

---

[251] WHO, *Female genital mutilation: Key Facts*, Feb. 3, 2020, available at https://www.who.int/news-room/fact-sheets/detail/female-genital-mutilation (accessed 5 September 2020).

[252] Nowa Omoigui, *Protest against Bill H22 Outlawing "FGM" in Nigeria* 1 (1) JOURNAL OF CULTURE AND AFRICAN WOMEN STUDIES (2001), available at http://www.jendajournal.com/vol1.1/omoigui.pdf (accessed 5 September 2020).

> It is not true that every type of genital ritual has the same implication or is practiced consistently across Nigeria or Africa. I am not aware of any Edo woman – for example – who has been properly circumcised whose clitoris or labia was amputated. What is removed is the prepuce – a small piece of the sheath that extends from the clitoris. That sheath has no sexual function and certainly no reproductive significance. It is the same sheath that is removed in males. In fact in many cases the 'removal' is symbolic – and is part of a traditional marriage ceremony.[253]

What Omoigui describes is the first portion of Type 1 FGR – that is, partial or total removal of the clitoral prepuce, known as "clitoridotomy" (or hoodectomy). This is a different procedure from clitoridectomy and is the type practiced in most parts of Southeastern Nigeria, including Enugu State. As has been asserted in a related context, contrary to popular claims, clitoridotomy is, "in fact, beneficial," in that by "allowing for maximum exposure of the clitoris, the procedure makes it possible for women to experience multiple, quicker, and more intense orgasms."[254] Therefore, to lump the procedure together with others that are harmful raises more questions than answers. After all, "sexual freedom—the right to enjoy sex without third-party interference—is a human right."[255]

III. FEMALE GENITAL RITUAL AND HARMFUL HEALTH CONSEQUENCES

There are two principal grounds upon which FGR is opposed, namely, as harboring harmful health consequences and as an infraction on the human rights of the victims. The focus of this section is on the first, adverse health consequences. The WHO has been the leading voice in opposing FGR on health grounds. A recent publication by the organisation states that the

---

253 *Id.*

254 Obiajulu Nnamuchi, *Circumcision or Mutilation - Voluntary or Forced Excision - Extricating the Ethical and Legal Issues in Female Genital Ritual,* 25 JOURNAL OF LAW & HEALTH 94 (2012), *citing* ELLEN GRUENBAUM, THE FEMALE CIRCUMCISION CONTROVERSY: AN ANTHROPOLOGICAL PERSPECTIVE 144 – 144 (2001)

255 Nnamuchi, *id*

health consequences of FGR vary according to the severity and type of the procedure.[256] It categorises health consequences resulting from FGR into three major groups, namely, immediate and long term as well as psychological complications. Immediate complications include severe pain, hemorrhage, genital tissue swelling, fever, infections such as tetanus, urinary problems and wound healing problems.[257] Others include injury to surrounding genital tissue, shock and death.[258]

Long-term complications include urinary problems (painful urination, urinary tract infections); vaginal problems (discharge, itching, bacterial vaginosis and other infections); menstrual problems (painful menstruations, difficulty in passing menstrual blood); scar tissue and keloid; sexual problems (pain during intercourse, decreased satisfaction and so forth).[259] Others include increased risk of childbirth complications (difficult delivery, excessive bleeding, caesarean section, need to resuscitate the baby) and newborn deaths; and need for later surgeries: for example, the sealing or narrowing of the vaginal opening (Type 3) may lead to the practice of cutting open the sealed vagina later to allow for sexual intercourse and childbirth (deinfibulation).[260] Psychological problems resulting from FGR include depression, anxiety, post-traumatic stress disorder, low self-esteem and so forth.[261]

It is on the strength of this long list of health complications that calls constantly arise, urging immediate cessation of the practice. Sociologist and legal scholar, Riane Eisler, laments that FGR "still kill, maim, and blight the physical and psychological health of millions of women and little children every year in many parts of Asia and Africa today."[262] Similarly, Susan Rich and colleague assert that FGR "has been practiced traditionally for centuries in sub-Saharan Africa. Customs, rituals, myths and taboos have perpetuated

---

256 WHO, note 15, *supra*.

257 *Id.*

258 *Id.*

259 *Id.*

260 *Id.*

261 *Id.*

262 Riane Eisler, *Human Rights: Toward an Integrated Theory of Action*, 9 HUMAN RIGHT QUARTERLY 287, 294 (1987).

the practice even though it has killed or maimed untold number of women and girls."[263] Quite an indictment, but does FGR really harbour this long list of serious health complications? Does the practice kill and main women and girls in practicing communities? To respond to this question, insight must be sought from three major studies.

The first is a 1999 study undertaken by Harvard public health scholar and former WHO consultant Carla Obermeyer—a project described as an "exhaustive review of the literature [on FGR]."[264] The study, which comprised 435 articles, including all sources in English and French,[265] was targeted at verifying whether the vast amount of literature on the adverse health consequences of FGR can be scientifically substantiated. This is Obermeyer's conclusion, following the review:

> [S]tudies that systematically investigate the sexual feelings of women and men in societies where genital surgeries are found are rare . . . and the scant information that is available calls into question the assertion that female genital surgeries are fundamentally antithetical to women's sexuality and incompatible with sexual enjoyment.[266]

The second, undertaken in 2005, was an update of Obermeyer earlier work on the subject.[267] Out of a total of 600 articles published between 1997 and 2005, 35 were chosen for review because, not only do they provide new data on the relationship between FGR and health and sexuality effects, they are also of

---

[263] Susan Rich & Stephanie Joyce, *Eradicating Female Genital Mutilation: Lesson for Donors, Wallace* Global Fund for a sustainable Future, Washington D.C. (no date given) 1, *cited in* Richard Shweder, *When Cultures Collide: Which Rights? Whose Tradition of Values? A Critique of the Global Anti-FGM Campaign*, in CHRISTOPHER EISGRUBER & ANDRAS SAJO EDS. GLOBAL JUSTICE AND THE BULWARKS OF LOCALISM: HUMAN RIGHTS IN CONTEXT 183 (2005).

[264] Carla Makhlouf Obermeyer, *Female Genital Surgeries: The Known, the Unknown, and the Unknowable* 13 MEDICAL ANTHROPOLOGY QUARTERLY 80 (1999).

[265] *Id.* at 81.

[266] *Id.* at 95

[267] Carla Makhlouf Obermeyer, *The Consequences of Female Circumcision for Health and Sexuality: An Update on the Evidence*, 7 CULTURE, HEALTH & SEXUALITY 445 (2005).

methodological acceptable quality.[268] Regarding sexuality, her review finds that "most of the existing studies suffer from conceptual and methodological shortcomings, and the available evidence does not support the hypotheses that circumcision destroys sexual function or precludes enjoyment of sexual relations."[269]

The third, a study similar to that of Obermeyer, published in 2010, had as its objective, to determine the psychological, social and sexual consequences of FGR.[270] The publication is the most recent serious meta-analysis of FGR publications till date. Importantly, of the 3,666 studies that were retrieved, only 17 met inclusion criteria,[271] namely, methodological quality.[272] Just two of the 17 studies were considered of high quality, five of moderate quality and ten of low quality.[273] Following review of the studies, which involved a total of 12,755 participants from nine different countries, the authors' conclusion was that, "[t]he low quality of the body of evidence precludes us from drawing conclusions regarding causality, and the evidence base is insufficient to draw solid conclusions about the psychological and social consequences of [FGR]."[274] This is quite an alarming conclusion; yet, neither this conclusion nor the study itself received global attention.

An apt conclusion to the discussion on the harmful health consequences of FGR is the work of Amede Obiora.[275] Describing herself as an "Igbo woman,"[276] perhaps to project her membership of a FGR-practicing culture and, hence, no stranger to the practice, Obiora bemoans the condemnatory disposition of most researchers even in the face of acute paucity of data

---

268 *Id.*

269 *Id.* at 443,459.

270 RIGMORE C. BERG, EVA DENISON & ATLE FRETHEIM, PSYCHOLOGICAL, SOCIAL AND SEXUAL CONSEQUENCES OF FEMALE GENITAL MUTILATION/CUTTING (FGM/C): A SYSTEMATIC REVIEW OF QUANTITATIVE STUDIES. REPORT FROM KUNNSKAPSSENTERET NR 13–2010 (2010).

271 *Id.* at 28.

272 Note that only cross-sectional and case-control studies were included. *Id.* at 26.

273 *Id.* at 36 – 37, 55 – 57.

274 *Id.* at 60.

275 L. Amede Obiora, *Bridges and Barricades: Rethinking Polemics and Intransigence in the Campaign against Female Circumcision* 47 CASE WESTERN LAW REVIEW 275 (1997).

276 *Id.*

regarding prevalence of the practice.[277] Her conclusion is that, in a bid to "orchestrate a 'sensation-value' and convey an outrageous impression of daily mutilation of millions of women," some of these very researchers:

> indulge in oppressive academic practices that range from crudity of methods, premature generalizations, and deductions of grand conclusions from scant and haphazard evidence to manipulative neglect of the distinctions between severe and negligible circumcision. Speculations are propagated as credible findings, and other findings fall short of vigorous analyses of the nuances and complexities.[278]

In the absence of scientifically rigorous studies demonstrating causality between the various conditions claimed to result from FGR, it would seem superfluous to decidedly focus on these claims as a fulcrum for eradication.

IV. FEMALE GENITAL RITUAL AND HUMAN RIGHTS

Does FGR offend human rights? The answer depends on who you ask. As intoned, however, by the spokesperson of the U.N. Secretary General, following the adoption of the U.N. Resolution on FGR in 2012, "[h]armful practices, such as genital mutilation . . . violate their [women's] fundamental rights."[279] But his assertion represents only one side of the debate. As postulated in a 2014 paper:

> This statement echoes an often repeated mantra in anti-FGR literature, namely, that the procedure violates the human rights of women in FGR societies, and that eradication campaign is geared toward protecting the human rights of these women against patriarchal tyranny and assault. Dressed in this garb of compassion and individual liberty, it becomes difficult to assail

---

[277] *Id.* at 325.

[278] *Id.* at 325.

[279] U.N. NEWS CENTER, Ban Welcomes UN General Assembly Resolution Eliminating Female Genital Mutilation, Dec. 21, 2012, available at http://www.un.org/apps/news/story.asp?NewsID=43839#.UslIf9JDtnk (accessed 5 Sept. 2020).

> the campaign since no one wishes to be seen as a defender of the indefensible, defending human rights infringement.[280]

Moreover, it might be instructive to juxtapose the views of eradication advocates against the opinion of the women themselves, those that voluntarily submitted to FGR. What is the latter's opinion? How do they view the procedure and the practice? This was the underlying rationale behind a study conducted by anthropologist, Rogaia Abusharaf, a question and answer session with women in Sudan, circumcised and are proud of the experience.[281] Unlike women in Southeastern Nigeria, these women underwent the most invasive type of FGR – infibulation. This response by one of the informant is particularly illuminating:

> Our mothers and grandmothers taught us that circumcision is very important for women and girls. I was given pharaonic circumcision when I was eight years . . . I still remember the operation being painful, but to this day I believe it is necessary . . . Female circumcision is a good custom because the removal of the external genitalia is necessary for girls . . . People try to do the sunna, but the real circumcision is pharaonic because a lot of doctors and some women are trying to teach people that their ways are wrong. Circumcision is what makes one a woman because by removing the clitoris, there is no way that her genital will look like a man's. The woman with a big clitoris is just like a man. How can a woman carry such a long organ between her legs and pretend that things are normal? That is why we say that pharaonic is good because after it is done the girl's genital area becomes very beautiful and smooth . . . For this reason, all my daughters were given pharaonic.

---

280 Obiajulu Nnamuchi, *United Nation's Resolution on Elimination of Female Genital Ritual: A Legitimate Response to a Human Rights Problem or What?* 33 MEDICINE AND LAW 97 (2014).

281 Rogaia Mustafa Abusharaf, *Virtuous Cuts: Female Genital Circumcision in an African Ontology*, 12 DIFFERENCES: JOURNAL OF FEMINIST CULTURAL STUDIES 112 (2001).

> None of them had any complications. Of course during the first days after the operation, they were not very comfortable. But when their wounds healed, they were fine. I continue to believe in it and I hope that people don't abandon it. It is an old Sudanese custom that should not be changed because without it, women's bodies are not as beautiful. A woman should do everything in her power to keep her body beautiful and she should do the same thing for her daughters, too.[282]

The verdict of other women in the study were equally reverential of the practice. Yet, eradication campaigners argue differently, which raises the question, whose human rights should we be concerned about?

The simple response is that if, as this paper contends, the goal of human rights is enablement of an environment that is conducive to the pursuit of individual good, it follows that the interest that matters is that of the primarily affected party. As human rights scholar, Jack Donnelly, postulates, a legitimate human rights framework must operate on the assumption that "people are best suited, and in any case are entitled, to choose the good life for themselves."[283] Differently put, "each and every human being possesses inherent right to make choices he or she believes maximizes his or her self-interests," and this "is not subject of any serious debate."[284]

Ability to make choices pertaining to one's life and activities is innate to humanity, a reason human rights law is built on the principle of individual autonomy. The word "autonomy" was derived from the Greek *autos* (self) and *nomos* (rule, governance or law), and originally used in description of self-rule or self-governance of Greek city states.[285] From this narrow socio-political beginning, the term has been broadened to include individuals and now encompasses concepts as diverse as "self-governance, liberty rights,

---

282 *Id.* at 123 – 124.

283 JACK DONNELLY, UNIVERSAL HUMAN RIGHTS IN THEORY AND PRACTICE 122 (2003).

284 Obiajulu Nnamuchi, *Hands Off My Pudendum: A Critique of Human Rights Approach to Female Genital Ritual* 15(2) QUINNIPIAC HEALTH LAW JOURNAL 267 (2012).

285 TOM L. BEAUCHAMP AND JAMES F. CHILDRESS, PRINCIPLES OF BIOMEDICAL ETHICS 57 – 58 (2001).

privacy, individual choice, freedom of the will, causing one's own behavior, and being one's own person."[286] The principle of autonomy projects the individual as an independent being, with a right to chart a path for his or her life, undisturbed by a third party. In other words, so long as the individual acts intentionally, rationally and competently, his choice of action or decision must be respected. As John Stuart Mill affirms:

> the only purpose for which power can be rightfully exercised over any member of a civilized community, against his will, is to prevent harm to others. His own good, either physical or moral, is not a sufficient warrant.[287]

Liberty restrictions, whether directed at an individual or a collectivity, which cannot be justified on this principle, is morally indefensible and an affront to human rights.

V. CONCLUSION

Referring to "informed consent" (in clinical practice), a concept derived from the principle of individual autonomy, this admonition was issued not long ago to clinicians who might be tempted by their own beliefs to override a competently expressed refusal:

> As a general principle, the unusual beliefs and choices of other persons should be tolerated if they pose no threat to other parties. The patient's preferences should be respected, even though they may appear mistaken to others.[288]

This admonition is not only applicable to practitioners of medicine, it is also a catechism of human rights. The right to self-determination entitles every rational adult to direct her actions to whichever end she wishes, and so long

---

[286] *Id.* at 58.

[287] JOHN STUART MILL, ON LIBERTY AND OTHER ESSAYS 10 (2010).

[288] ALBERT JONSEN, MARK SIEGLER, AND WILLIAM J. WINSLADE, CLINICAL ETHICS: A PRACTICAL APPROACH TO ETHICAL DECISIONS IN CLINICAL MEDICINE 74 (2006).

as the exercise of this right does not detrimentally impact a third party, there will be no legitimate basis to interfere. Granted that some expressions of preferences might appear odd, barbaric or outrightly bizarre to others, such expressions should be accommodated in a pluralistic society. The mantra should be "live and let live," not intolerance or superciliousness. Toleration of diversity of beliefs and practices is the glue that hold (or should hold) pluralistic societies together regardless of geography. Community cohesion, solidarity and stability requires accommodating fiercely disparate views, especially of action toward oneself and which constitutes no harm to a third party. It is this accommodation that is sought regarding the prohibitory tentacles of section 9 of the Enugu State VAPP Law regarding FGR.